LOUISIANA
Postmistress and Postmaster Appointments

20 June 1866 to
17 November 1931

Harry F. Dill

HERITAGE BOOKS
2011

HERITAGE BOOKS
AN IMPRINT OF HERITAGE BOOKS, INC.

Books, CDs, and more—Worldwide

For our listing of thousands of titles see our website
at
www.HeritageBooks.com

Published 2011 by
HERITAGE BOOKS, INC.
Publishing Division
100 Railroad Ave. #104
Westminster, Maryland 21157

Other books by the author:

Some Slaveholders and Their Slaves, Union Parish, Louisiana, 1839–1865
Harry F. Dill and William Simpson

African American Inhabitants of Rapides Parish, Louisiana: 15 June–4 Sept 1870

Marriages and Deaths from The Caucasian, *Shreveport, Louisiana, 1903–1913*

Appointments of Postmasters in Louisiana, 12 January 1827–28 December 1892

The Underground Railroad and the Picayune *Connection*

International Standard Book Numbers
Paperbound: 978-0-7884-5332-8
Clothbound: 978-0-7884-8807-8

Table of Contents

Preface

Geneologists seeking ancestors who resided in Louisiana parishes in this book have an unusual source. Finding female forebears who served as postmistresses could offer a special highlight for family historians.

Also, the discovery that a male relative actually had charge of a post office should lend novelty to any family's written account of descent.

Appointments as postmasters began in 1775 when our fledgling Congress named Benjamin Franklin as our first Postmaster. In 1789, George Washington appointed Samuel Osgood as the first Postmaster General, fourteen years after Benjamin's tenure (1775-1776).

Congress ruled in 1836 that appointments must be made by the President and confirmed by the Senate at post offices where annual salary of an appointee exceeded the sum of $1,000.00. To identify those thus appointed, this book has emphasized them as, (Pres & Sen).

The statuary requirement for Presidential and Senate confirmation was removed by Congress. The Postal Reorganization Act of 1970 halted all appointments by the Postmaster General. Since then, appointments have been effected on merit alone.

Material in this book, "Louisiana Postmistress and Postmaster Appointments 20 June 1866-17 November 1931" was extracted from a reel of microfilm produced by National Archives, Washington, DC, in 1968 from original, handwritten post office records.

POST OFFICE
LOCATIONS

POSTMASTER AND
APPOINTMENT DATES

AVOYELLES PARISH, LOUISIANA

Big Bend

John Everett 25 Oct 1867
James T Griffin 7 Nov 1881
William Branch Marshall 15 Nov 1882
Mary P Spurlock 12 Nov 1883
James T Griffin 3 Oct 1888
Mrs Effa S Griffin 21 Aug 1889
Clint Pearce 11 Jun 1891
David Demaree 6 Sep 1893
Amelia Marcotte 3 Oct 1896
Mrs Emma V Marshall 26 Jan 1901
John F Archdekin 3 Oct 1918
Byron F Lemoine 27 Apr 1920

Boboc

Octavia A Jeansonne 15 Feb 1895
Louis Hooter 19 Nov 1901
William D Travasos 26 Jul 1902

Bordelonville

Remie Bordelon 20 Jan 1870
Remie Bordelon 20 Jun 1896
Etta C Firment 17 Jan 1919

Bunkie

Thomas B Kimbro 26 Jan 1883
Louis W Anderson 16 Apr 1884
John D Earnest 30 Aug 1889
Levi P Carter 21 Dec 1897
Levi P Carter 18 Feb 1904 (Pres & Sen)
Levi P Carter 14 May 1908 (Pres & Sen)
Levi P Carter 12 Jun 1912 (Pres & Sen)
Ewell West 1 Sep 19616 (Pres & Sen)
Levi P Carter 19 May 1922

Levi P Carter 28 May 1926 (Pres & Sen)
Levi P Carter 20 May 1930 (Pres & Sen)

Centerpoint
Alexander S Baker 14 Dec 1891
Joseph R Simmons 1 Feb 1897
John R McNeal 29 Jan 1917
Zoe E McNeal 7 Dec 1917
Cloyce M McNeal 1 Feb 1927

Cottonport[1]
Gervais A Bordelon 7 Mar 1872
John T Nelson 17 Mar 1875
Avit Lemoine 17 Dec 1878
Firmin Serenne 12 May 1880
Serge Callegori 25 Oct 1880
Oscar Lemoine 23 Jan 1884
Louis F Callegori 30 Apr 1886
Emile Gauthier 4 Jan 1898
Joseph R Ducote 11 May 1904
Leo J Roth 12 Nov 1904
Leo J Roth 1 Jan 1911 (Pres & Sen)
Ulysses J Marcotte 24 Feb 1915
Ulysses J Marcotte 11 Jul 1915 (Pres & Sen)
Ulysses J Marcotte 23 Jan 1917 (Pres & Sen)
Joseph D Hebert 20 Dec 1921 (Pres & Sen)
Joseph D Hebert 12 Jan 1926 (Pres & Sen)
Joseph D Hebert 1 Feb 1930

Egg Bend
Archibald D Derivas 21 May 1878
Francois M Joffrion 8 Feb 1881
Jules E Didier 11 Apr 1888
Mrs Cora Clara Frank Didier 31 Jul 1888
Jules Didier 25 Jan 1899
John H Chauffepied 5 May 1903
John H Chauffepied 1 Feb 1907
William D Smith 25 Nov 1910
John H Chauffepied 11 Nov 1911
Martin M LaComb 5 Nov 1918

Eola
Daniel B Hudson 14 Nov 1881

---

[1] Disc 23 Jan 1875
Reest 17 Dec 1878

William C Scott 24 May 1884
Mrs Laura F Hudson 21 Jan 1885
Daniel B Hudson 26 Jul 1888
M A Wade 18 Nov 1889
(Rescinded 24 Dec 1889)
George B Hudson 2 Apr 1896

Evergreen
Joseph Cappel 3 Jan 1870
Isaac C Johnson 27 Dec 1879
John D Earnest 31 Jan 1887
Isaac C Johnson 23 Dec 1888
Clara Toon 15 Jun 1890
Calvin D Cappel 10 Jul 1894
Genie Simmons 3 Feb 1903

Green Stone
Eugene C Hayes 4 Feb 1890
Eugene C Hayes 7 Feb 1893

Haasville
A Marshall Haas 6 Jul 1904
J Charles Bostick 17 May 1906
A Marshall Haas 25 Mar 1909

Simmesport
Mrs Azema Leigh 23 Jun 1871
John S Hosea 18 Sep 1873
Walter T Lansdell 22 Jun 1883
Thomas L Berand 30 Nov 1883
William H Thompson 10 Apr 1884
Thomas S Denson 22 Oct 1890
Albert C Simmonds 9 June 1900
Charles M Denny 18 May 1903
Noel Norwood 5 Mar 1909
Alfred L Dupon 5 Dec 1916

Tilden[2]
Jefferson D Robinson 16 Dec 1880
Walter F Coyle 30 Dec 1881
Charles Smith 18 Dec 1882
Robert H Baker 20 Feb 1883

---

[2] Disc 15 May 1909

James O E Cain 14 Jan 1884
James K Bond 30 Apr 1886
Mrs Mary A Bond 2 May 1888

Couvillon
L L Gauthier 7 Jul 1882
Albert F Collins 2 Jul 1903

Longbridge
Ernest B Coco 26 Jul 1893
Landry L Bordelon 10 May 1903
Joseph P Cazale 17 June 1914

Voorhies
Etienne O Voorhies 10 Feb 1894
Eugene C Voorhies 17 Jul 1903
Eugene Couvillon 30 Jul 1903
Jules F Coco 9 Jul 1907

Norma
Mrs Cora Jeansonne 5 July 1894
Walter F Couvillon 27 Aug 1897
Pierre N Conlan 12 Jan 1898
Hattie Berlin 21 Aug 1901
S A Barnard 23 Feb 1904

Belleville
C Bielkiewicz 6 Apr 1895
Henry Bielkiewicz 24 Apr 1895
Alphonse M Voinche 5 Jul 1902

Woodside
William J Bentley 13 Mar 1878
Victor J Oplalek 18 May 1870
William J Bentley 27 Jan 1882
Lena Callahan 13 Jul 1895
Willa H White 27 Aug 1897
Paul W Lafleur 30 Mar 1910
A Phonlin Lafleur 5 Apr 1915
William P Paxton 6 Oct 1916
Corinne C Hamilton 6 Oct 1920
Josey P Foley 23 Jun 1926
Ozia Langlaid 11 Feb 1927

Goudeau

Adolph A Goudeau 19 Sep 1895
Ada E Goudeau 10 Jan 1925

Kleinewood[3]
Bettison W Blakewood 22 May 1896
Wilford B Marcotte 8 Aug 1898
Dan W Hart 17 Jul 1899
Eldred Blackwood 6 Feb 1902
Elder G Blackwood 11 Oct 1913

Effie
Benjamin F Darlington 13 Apr 1898
Pauline J Daniel 26 Dec 1911
Willie H Ryland 19 Mar 1919

Vick
Mrs Elizabeth M Lelland 29 Nov 1898
Joseph A Berlin 23 Oct 1899
Nicholas J Berlin 11 Jul 1904
Mary B Berlin 26 Jun 1914
Oren Sayles 20 Jan 1926
Ovada G Sayles 11 Mar 1931

Hickory[4]
Gustave P Gremillion 20 Feb 1899
Leon B Gremillion 22 Aug 1906

Hamburg
Edward D Coco 15 Aug 1888
Francis M Pavey 19 Dec 1890
Olivier P Couvillon 13 May 1922

Mansura
David Siess 20 Jun 1866
Jean Pride Dormas 30 Dec 1881
Pierre A Durand 5 Oct 1883
Tesca Roy 27 Jun 1893
David Siess 27 Aug 1897
Pierre A Durand 17 Oct 1899
Josephine Gaspard 5 Jun 1900
Sydonie Regard 24 Sep 1901
Edward A Drouin 15 May 1903

---

[3] Disc 14 Jun 1919
[4] Disc 8 Feb 1907

Harry J Siess 6 June 1907
Edward A Drouin 22 May 1914
Edward A Drouin 1 Apr 1919 (Pres & Sen)
Edward A Drouin 11 Feb 1920 (Pres & Sen)
Edward A Drouin 24 Apr 1923 (Pres & Sen)
Edward A Drouin 2 May 1928

Marksville

George L Mayer 11 Apr 1871
Henry Dupuy 1 Jun 1874
Charles F Huesman 2 Feb 1881
Henry Dupuy 15 Aug 1883
George L Mayer 18 Feb 1887
James M Edwards 22 May 1889
Oscar B DeBellvue 16 Apr 1891
Benjamin F Edwards 1 Jul 1891
Mrs Mary H Hall 9 Feb 1894
Jeanne Bize 31 Mar 1899
Jeanne Dupuy 7 Oct 1899
Henry Dupuy 22 May 1901
Henry C Edwards 26 Feb 1903
Henry C Edwards 14 May 1908
B F Edwards 1 May 1911 (Pres & Sen)
Lester L Bordelon 4 Oct 1913 (Pres & Sen)
Lu J Couvillon 31 Jul 1916
Lester L Bordelon 23 Jan 1917
Lester L Bordelon 8 Nov 1921
Mrs Edwin L Lafargue 16 Dec 1925
Mrs Edwin L Lafargue 18 Dec 1929

Milburn

William C Townsend 23 Nov 1889
Walter Seales 15 Feb 1905
Toulman T Sandefur 12 Mar 1907

Moureauville

James A Boyer 30 Jul 1866
Alonzo L Boyer 1 Jul 1874
Jacques A Boyer 12 Mar 1875
Alonzo L Boyer 2 Aug 1882
Alphonze J Escude 2 Feb 1888
Gervais A Bordelon 3 Oct 1888
Thomas L Lemoine 15 Jun 1893
Alonzo L Boyer 24 Dec 1897
Sambola L Couvillion 15 May 1914

Henry F Couvillion 16 Mar 1936

Odenburg[5]
>Jefferson Hetherwick 22 Apr 1885
>John D Oden 15 Feb 1890
>Gordon Morgan 4 Apr 1904
>Clarence Hetherwick 14 Apr 1904
>William W Watkins 23 Jun 1909
>Gordon Morgon 5 May 1912
>William C Gordon 14 Apr 1915
>Walthall B Gordon 12 Aug 1922
>Joseph H Rabalais 12 Feb 1924

Plaucheville[6]
>F M Gremillion 10 May 1880
>Jean V Plauche 28 Jul 1890
>Richard H Cox 24 Jan 1891
>Richard H Cox 9 Mar 1892
>Elizabeth J Fanning 28 Jul 1893
>Cyriaque B Plauche 10 Jul 1898
>Marcelina Chenvert 20 Oct 1898
>Maise E Chenvert 19 May 1910
>Maise E Chenvert 31 Jun 1927
>Maise E Chenvert 19 Dec 1927 (Pres & Sen)
>Maise E Chenvert 8 Jul 1928 (Pres & Sen)

Red Fish
>William R Howard 11 May 1888
>Henry C Perkins 11 Sep 1888
>William D Merrick 24 Feb 1905
>Isabelle Jackson 7 Mar 1921
>Thomas J Perkins 26 Jul 1924
>Simon Holden 7 Mar 1925

Bettevy[7]
>Miche Bettevy 27 May 1899

Holmesville
>Walker A Ardenhead 14 Dec 1868

---

[5] Disc 1 Sep 1929
[6] Disc 23 Jun 1880
   Reest 28 Jul 1890
[7] Disc 17 Nov 1899

Gertrude A Ardenhead 8 May 1877
Daniel B Hudson 3 May 1880

Mordoc
Winburn L Chafin 3 Oct 1888
Traville E Jeansonne 21 Mar 1892

Corner
Augustin F Bonnett 7 Apr 1886

Meyersville
Mrs Esther Alexander 2 Jun 1888

Cassandra[8]
Montillion J Ryland 22 Nov 1871

Tiger Bend
Alexander M Haas 18 Dec 1879

Heuffpower[9]
Thomas J Heard 3 Jun 1872

Moncla
Ernest Moncla 17 Nov 1899
Constant J Moncla 28 Jul 1916
Louis E Moncla 18 Jun 1919
Laura Moncla 16 Feb 1922

Sarah[10]
Joseph S Simmons 15 Aug 1901

Hessmer
Stephen A Bernard 10 Mar 1904
Louis W Carpenter 29 Dec 1904
Thomas J Carruth (No date shown)

Hydrophilia[11]
Joseph J Domar 29 Aug 1905

Florence[12]

---

[8] Disc 6 Jun 1879
[9] Disc 22 Feb 1875
[10] Disc 14 Feb 1910
[11] Disc 27 Apr 1908
[12] Disc 4 May 1906

Elisha Attaway 8 Sep 1905

North Point[13]
    Joseph F Busnaman 4 Aug 1910

Gold Dust
    James V Lawther 24 Jan 1906
    William Lawther 25 Sep 1925
    Taulman T Sandefer 19 May 1916

Belledean
    William T Simmons 20 May 1909
    Tempey Laborde 20 Oct 1913
    Tempey Laborde 19 May 1916

Naples[14]
    Thomas J Carruth 5 Apr 1911
    Carey D Wren 6 Jul 1914
    Isidore Rothchild 3 Jul 1917

Rexmire[15]
    Sam E Lingard 3 Oct 1913
    R E Williams 27 Jul 1915

Reynolds[16]
    David W Raynolds 10 May 1911

Clots
    John H Chauffepied 11 Nov 1911
    Lillie Scroggs 13 Jun 1918
    Martin M LaComb 5 Nov 1918

Eola
    Daniel B Hudson 14 Nov 1881
    William C Scott 24 May 1884
    Mrs Laura F Hudson 21 Jan 1885
    Daniel B Hudson 26 Jul 1888

---

[13] Disc 31 Aug 1912
[14] Disc 28 Feb 1919
[15] Disc 15 Oct 1927
[16] Disc 15 Jun 1929

POST OFFICE LOCATIONS	POSTMASTER AND APPOINTMENT DATES

CALCASIEU PARISH, LOUISIANA

Hickory Flat[17]
 Abner Cole 12 Sep 1880
 Louis Doucet 14 Sep 1880
 Seth B Singleton 9 Jun 1883
 Joseph Chenier 6 Feb 1884
 Milton Bihm 11 Jun 1884
 James Cole 18 Oct 1892

Nibbet's Bluff[18]
 Samuel A Fairchild 21 Apr 1873

Rose Bluff[19]
 Oliver R Moss 7 Jun 1873

Wood's Bluff[20]
 Jerisan Broussard 12 Jun 1873

Barnes Creek[21]
 Hiram C Lyles 29 Oct 1874
 Henry A Williams 4 May 1875

Dry Creek
 Levi A Miller 3 Nov 1874
 George W Heard 4 Jan 1883
 Norman J Perry 23 Aug 1891
 Joseph T Kent 29 Apr 1892

---

[17] Disc 6 Feb 1880
 Reest 12 Apr 1880
[18] Disc 3 Jan 1884
[19] Disc 5 Mar 1883
[20] Disc 12 Sep 1873
[21] Disc 19 Jun 1876

Big Woods
>Benjamin B Saxon 22 Jun 2874
>David A Lyons 27 Jun 1876
>George W Roberts 14 Feb 1877

West Fork[22]
>Allen J Perkins 21 Sep 1874
>James K Perkins 4 May 1875

Lyons [23]
>John F Davidson 8 Aug 1877

Meadows
>Isaac S Meadows 11 Dec 1879
>Laban Wingate 29 Feb 1884
>Henry A Knight 9 Feb 1885

Hardy[24]
>Hardy C Gill 24 Oct 1882

Sabine Station
>Joseph H Jackson 7 Nov 1883
>Edwin F M Fairchild 24 May 1887
>James H Jackson 30 Sep 1889

Bryan
>William F Perkins 11 Aug 1885
>Fredericka A Perkins 4 Dec 1888

Bond
>John Bond 22 Jul 1895
>W W Johnson 28 Oct 1898
>William E Bond 11 Sep 1899

Bear
>Joseph W Barrow 18 Feb 1887
>John Hill 24 Jan 1891
>William M Young 14 Sep 1891
>William J Mitchell 12 Jul 1894
>James D Willar 12 Oct 1901

---

[22] Disc 19 Jul 1876
[23] Disc 3 Sep 1878
[24] Disc 7 Jan 1884

Beckworth

    William R Davis 18 Feb 1887
    Sulliano Slayclaw 22 Jun 1895

Burissa

    George H Ford 7 Jun 1887
    George H Ford 1 Oct 1895

Calcasieu[25]

    August Johnson 8 Aug 1880
    John J Drost 30 Dec 1897
    John J Drost 14 Dec 1901
    Erastus C Sofer 19 Oct 1907
    Arcilla A Tucker 7 Jan 1916
    Robert L Parks 16 Sep 1916

Canton

    James N Strother 30 Sep 1886
    Ernest Lafleur 2 Apr 1891
    John L Lyons 25 Apr 1899
    Dewitt C Powell 13 Jul 1903
    Yieve O Reed 23 Feb 1908

China

    William Jackson 6 Jul 1880
    Miss Lucinda Jackson 18Aug 1880
    Benjamin F Car 30 Jan 1888
    Isaac Griffith 5 May 1888
    Frank McVey 26 Feb 1892
    Arthur H Anderson 12 Jun 1895
    Marquis D Sutherlin 21 Mar 1904
    Willis W Tuffer 3 Sep 1910
    Arthur H Anderson 14 Oct 1917

Edgerly

    John F Davidson 2 Oct 1880
    Edward J Fairchild 23 Mar 1888
    Edward J Fairchild 14 May 1891
    Henry B Reed 20 Mar 1901
    John C Chesson 23 Apr 1910

Easterly

    Michael Funk 17 Jun 1889

---

[25] Disc 15 Nov 1916

Samuel A Shaver 18 May 1894

Iona

Edward L Hauck 17 Feb 1903
John Storer 26 Jul 1905
Fidello C Baker 25 Nov 1908

Gay

William F Fargue 18 Feb 1887

Iola

Thomas E Wingate 26 Feb 1887
Samuel Biven 17 Apr 1888

Welch

Coleman D Welch 18 Sep 1883
Lee E Robinson 23 Aug 1889
Mrs Fredericka A Perkins 23 Nov 1889
Mrs Annie B Good 15 Feb 1896
Willis A Pitre 17 Mar 1899
Willis A Pitre 21 Mar 1900 (Pres & Sen)
Arthur G Wachsen 28 Dec 1901
James L Williams 26 Sep 1904
Henry E Carter 23 Jul 1908
Ector R Gammage 3 Mar 1909
Ector R Gammage 1 Apr 1910 (Pres & Sen)
Samuel A Gandy 19 Mar 1914
Samuel A Gandy 5 Sep 1914
Samuel A Gandy 5 Sep 1918 (Pres & Sen)
Felix L LeBlanc 11 Feb 1920 (Pres & Sen)
Ector R Gammage 19 Mar 1924 (Pres & Sen)

Fenton

Silas Fenton 16 May 1892
Fidello C Baker 3 Feb 1906
Dallas H Reeves 10 Mar 1908

Kinder

Charles T Higgins 12 Jul 1892
J M Garrett 26 Feb 1895
Patrick E Moore 24 May 1899
Richard E Oden 5 Dec 1902
William Navils 12 Mar 1907
Richard E Oden 2 Mar 1908

Grant

James A Grant 3 Jul 1894
Samuel W B Colvin 9 Jul 1897
James A Baggett 3 Apr 1899
Robert E Johnson 12 Jun 1901
James A Grant 9 Nov 1909

Bundick

Covington J Sigler 12 Mar 1894
John E Parker 11 Dec 1901

Miersburg

Elias Miers 12 May 1894

Edgewood

Henry V Hall 19 Sep 1895
Fleming F Smith Jr 27 Aug 1897
George F Goss 28 Apr 1898

Roanoke

Samuel A Shaver 19 Mar 1895
Joseph M Booze 24 Apr 1895
William T Hutcheson 28 Apr 1898
Joseph M Booze 26 Mar 1901
William R Eiber 24 Apr 1905
Bert T Wait 25 Jan 1910
Lula Pierce 18 Feb 1913
Hazel V Pierce 10 Jan 1928

Jacksonville[26]

James H Jackson 3 Apr 1890
Perry L Langdon 31 Jan 1894
Perry L Langdon 19 Sep 1911

Jennings

Andrew D McFarlain 29 Nov 1880
Delino Deronen 11 Aug 1885
Andew D McFarlain 17 May 1889
John H Roberts 17 Jun 1889
Albert F Deronen 18 May 1893
Albert F Deronen 1 Oct 1896 (Pres & Sen)
Albert F Deronen 12 Jan 1897

---

[26] Disc 30 Sep 1913

14

Horace S Feree 16 Jun 1901
Edward J Hall 19 Aug 1904 (Pres)
Edward J Hall 12 Dec 1904 (Pres & Sen)

Lakassine[27]
Pierre A Hebert 7 Dec 1874

Lacasine[28]
Coleman D Welch 31 Mar 1880
Louis Lorrain 9 Feb 1885
Villore V Verret 22 Sep 1892
Prosper Verrett 21 Aug 1895

Lake Arthur
Delino Deronen 24 May 1870
Felix Laurents 13 Aug 1887
Alexander P Hebert 16 Apr 1888
Joseph H Shively 18 Nov 1889
Maria Agnes Lee 5 Mar 1891
Clement W Gorman 10 Oct 1891
Henry B Wright 5 Oct 1892
Charles W Kingery 12 Jun 1895
Catherine Kingery 27 Aug 1899
Marcus N Limbocker 26 Sep 1901

Lake Charles
Charvey Barbe 13 Aug 1869
William Meyer 13 Apr 1872
Daniel H Reese 16 Nov 1876
William D Mearns 4 Jun 1879
W H Haskell 24 Feb 1881
J B Kirman 29 Aug 1881 (Declined)
Thomas B Ferren 12 Sep 1881
William D Mearns 26 Feb 1883 (Pres & Sen)
Mary J Leveque 12 Jan 1886 (Pres & Sen)
Dennis M Foster 11 Feb 1890 (Pres & Sen)
James P Geary 20 Apr 1893
James P Geary 19 Sep 1893 (Pres & Sen)
James M Mason 27 Jul 1897 (Pres & Sen)
James M Mason 22 Jul 1898

---

[27] Disc 24 Aug 1877
[28] Late Lakassine

George H Woolman 18 Apr 1899 (Pres)
George H Woolman 14 Dec 1899 (Pres & Sen)
James S Thompson 14 Feb 1901
James S Thompson 1 Mar 1905
Tolbert J Wakefield 14 Jun 1909 (Pres & Sen)
Harry J Geary 17 Jun 1913 (Pres & Sen)
Harry J Geary 21 Jul 1917 (Pres & Sen)
Dennis M Foster Jr 29 Mar 1922 (Pres & Sen)
Dennis M Foster Jr 9 Apr 1926 (Pres & Sen)
Dennis M Foster Jr 2 May 1930 (Pres & Sen)

Loretta

Ethelbert L Cannon 1 Feb 1883
Ethelbert L Cannon 21 May 1900

Merryville

Moses E Frazar 30 Nov 1881
James E McMahon 14 Feb 1889
Thomas E Hyatt 20 May 1900
James E M Hennigan 23 Sep 1903
August P Windham 21 Jan 1905

Mystic

John T Davidson 15 May 1890
Thomas W Davidson 27 Dec 1897
Mrs C M Davidson 31 Aug 1900
Eardean T Hyatt 2 May 1902
Benjamin F Davidson 23 Apr 1908
Walter F Berthune 12 Mar 1909
James E Thomas 29 Mar 1910
Gilbert F Hennigan 29 Nov 1910
Ocier W Young 20 Nov 1911
Estelle Herford 13 Jun 1913

Oaklin Spring

George Wilcocks 12 Jan 1886
Joseph Chenier 8 Jun 1888
Samuel C Poole 25 Nov 1891
Juliette Wilcox 11 Jan 1896
Eugene Hewitt 11 Feb 1896
Joseph Chenier 17 Nov 1899

Oberlin

Charles Powers 16 Apr 1890
Harvey L Rice 22 Sep 1890

16

Lula M Evans 25 Oct 1890
Harvey L Rice 22 Dec 1890
Elizabeth A Paul 24 Jul 1891
Norman D Perry 15 Nov 1892
Edward S Clements 25 Sep 1896
Mary C Cary 20 Jul 1898
Luc DeDoux 14 Aug 1901
Thomas N Hewitt 24 Aug 1905
Joseph A Darbonne 17 Feb 1906
Joseph Chenier 20 Jun 1907
Anthony Cole 28 Feb 1908
Auletus L Pitts 12 Feb 1909

Pearl

Joseph J Kingery 4 May 1883
Samson R Kingery 21 Aug 1891
Joseph J Kingery 1 Jul 1897
Anthony Cole 28 Jul 1901
David C Creel 26 April 1902
Frances L Nixon 31 Jan 1907

Philip's Bluff[29]

Henry F Myers 26 Jul 1876
Edgar L Riddick 11 Jun 1877
Eych Clement 16 Jul 1878
Martha A E Moore 9 Oct 1884
James J Baker 28 Sep 1892

Pine Hill

James D Standfield 4 Feb 1889
Larkin M Mims 1 Apr 1890
Henry M Brown 3 Oct 1895
Octave Gaidry 13 Jul 1896
Larkin M Mims 1 Apr 1898

Simmons

Albert Burnett 24 Mar 1890
Albert Burnett 13 Sep 1895

Soileau

James Cole 5 Oct 1880
Joseph D Lafleur 7 May 1888

---

[29] Disc 21 Jan 1878
Reest 16 Jul 1878

William L Davis 22 Aug 1888
Jethro Thompson 16 Oct 1889
Charles W Staneart 6 Aug 1890
Johann Simon 15 Dec 1894
Abbie Ford 25 Jul 1895
Mrs Abbie Soileau 19 Dec 1896

Sulphur

Margaret B Lewis 22 May 1892
John T Henning 2 Mar 1895
James Hillebrandt 26 Dec 1901
George E Leray 18 Mar 1903
Erastus Vincent 12 Nov 1904
Minnie M Parsons 10 Aug 1905
Mrs Minnie A Stine 8 Nov 1907
John L Drost 15 Mar 1909
John L Drost 6 Jul 1910 (Pres & Sen)
John L Drost 13 Jul 1911
Mrs A A Drost 4 Dec 1912
H Schindler 28 Apr 1913 (Pres & Sen)
H Schindler 21 Jul 1917 (Pres & Sen)
Frank Granger 14 Feb 1922
James R Coplen 19 Apr 1922 (Pres & Sen)
Mrs Grover S Miller 31 Mar 1928
Eugene A Tonniette 13 Jul 1929 (Pres & Sen)

Sulphur City[30]

Eli A Perkins 2 Dec 1880
Frederick S Schinkoth 15 Feb 1884
John A Vincent 2 Feb 1885
John T Hennigan 1 Feb 1886

Pinchburg

Louis E Mazilly 26 Aug 1880
Shivene S Andues 4 Feb 1886
Edward B Wright 29 Jul 1886
Edward B Wright 1 Sep 1886

West Lake

Fredericka A Perkins 31 Jan 1889
Fredericka A Perkins 23 Nov 1889
Ector R Gammage 17 May 1928

---

[30] Disc 31 Jul 1884
Reest 5 Feb 1885

Sugartown
Henry C Faquhar 28 Oct 1873
George W Richardson 10 Jul 1885
Neal Roberts 24 Jan 1901
Mollie Iles 9 Jan 1908

Ten Mile
Archey C R Turner 21 Sep 1886
James I Hamilton 12 Mar 1891
May Hamilton 20 Feb 1904
Marshall A Simmons 22 Sep 1906
William J Dowies 26 Oct 1907

The Bay
Hugh B Thompson 9 Oct 1876
William T Dunn 21 Dec 1890
William T Dunn 27 Dec 1893

Thompson
Ignace Rodriques 10 Jul 1888
Charles J Miles 20 Aug 1894

Ledoux
Ozette Ledoux 25 Apr 1888

Vincent
Nathaniel Vincent 12 Aug 1887
Nathaniel Vincent 12 Aug 1900
A J West 28 Mar 1901
Charles Pearson 8 Nov 1907

Vinton
Ezekial P Melwick 10 Sep 1888
Benjamin T Stockwell 27 Aug 1893
Ashley B Hall 13 Feb 1895
Lulu U Roderick 21 Jan 1907
Lulu U Roderick 1 Jan 1912 (Pres)
Given C Roderick 12 Jan 1915
Henry J Nelson 15 Feb 1915 (Pres & Sen)
Henry J Nelson 28 Jul 1919 (Pres & Sen)
Samuel A Fairchild 8 Jan 1924 (Pres & Sen)
Samuel A Fairchild 2 May 1928 (Pres & Sen)

Iowa
>Mrs Eliza A Williamson 24 Mar 1888
>Elmer J Johnson 22 Aug 1888
>James Storer 22 Oct 1889

Serpent
>Sevrin Langley 18 May 1886
>Octave Gaidry 13 Oct 1891

Hellinger[31]
>Joseph Hellinger 2 Jul 1886

Fields
>Joseph C Craddock 6 Sep 1895
>William J Sanders 24 Mar 1903
>James G Beard 8 Aug 1907
>William A Holbrook 13 Aug 1908
>Harvey C Kellis 13 Apr 1909

Oakdale
>William Perkins 3 Jul 1898
>Mrs Ophelia E Perkins 14 Mar 1900
>William Hargrave 26 Oct 1906

Elton
>Isaac M Henderson 15 Jun 1896
>Willie A Brown 1 Nov 1909
>Hugh B Curry 30 Apr 1910

Wellborn
>William B Wellborn 19 Feb 1897
>H C Hall 3 Jul 1899

Gillis
>Cyrus W Gillis 26 May 1898
>Samuel R Kingery 31 May 1899
>John D Haves 20 Oct 1903
>Samuel Smart 16 Jun 1904
>William A Walsh 29 Jan 1907
>Levi Robbins Jr 7 Dec 1907
>Theodosia Rollins 28 Mar 1918
>Blance M Jones 19 Jun 1923

---

[31] Disc 20 Sep 1887

20

Pawnee

George W Brown 26 Jul 1897
Thomas S Dunnham 28 Sep 1903
Dudley H Veal 1 Jan 1904
John Fredericks 1 Jun 1906
Frank H Heins 11 Dec 1906

Lowry

Absalom G Murray 1 Mar 1898
Peter K Miller 7 Mar 1903
Gilbert R Molloy 24 Nov 1905
Absalom G Murray 19 Dec 1906
Peter P Unkel 27 May 1907

DeQuincy

Amos Wheeler 14 Mar 1898
Fleming F Smith 22 Aug 1898
Herman J Jessen 17 Aug 1900
Drew D Herford 11 Feb 1901
Lucy L Foster 22 Aug 1904
George W Smith 8 Mar 1907 (Pres & Sen)
George W Smith 1 Jul 1912 (Pres & Sen)
Hugo Naegele 8 Aug 1912
Thomas J Perkins 2 Nov 1912 (Pres & Sen)
Thomas J Perkins 2 Jul 1913 (Pres & Sen)
Lucy L Tenish 14 Jul 1914
Thomas J Perkins 31 Jan 1918 (Pres & Sen)
Warren W Grimes 21 Jan 1922
Alice L Gailbraith 1 Jul 1922 (Pres & Sen)
William T Kent 6 Apr 1931 (Pres)

Singer

Aaron P Cosand 22 Aug 1898
John E Moore 4 Jan 1901
Aaron P Cosand 23 Sep 1904
Thomas W Davidson 19 Feb 1906

Davis Mills

William E Fletcher 10 May 1898
Leah Lewis 14 Jul 1902

Starks

John Faxon 13 May 1898
Robert R Faxon 10 Jul 1902
Mitchell M Wood 19 Jan 1906

William O Ridgway 12 Jul 1906
Julius K Fairly 5 Aug 1909
Varice Clark 2 Oct 1912
Harmon D Foster 20 Mar 1915
Ernest D Batchelor 2 Nov 1921

Woodburg

Napoleon B Wood 20 Sep 1898
Jack Courmier 27 Feb 1902
J Lee Herford 16 Jun 1903
William T Herron 8 Mar 1905

DeRidder

Elias Miers 25 Jan 1899
Willie H Knight 11 Sep 1899
Henry E Hall 26 Dec 1901
Henry E Sweet 2 Jun 1904
Henry E Sweet 23 Feb 1905 (Pres & Sen)
Cora Shapless 25 Apr 1905 (Pres)

LeBlanc

Joseph M LeBlanc 20 Dec 1899
Martha White 31 Dec 1903
Joseph G White 6 Jun 1907

Bine

Preston P Greene 7 Feb 1900

Seale

Albert B Seale 20 Feb 1900
Albert B Seale 12 Feb 1901

Glen

Thomas C Austin 5 Mar 1900
Jacob Stozle 21 Jan 1902
John H Doescher 27 May 1903

Oran

Henry D Henderson 20 May 1900

Ikeville

Isaac Doiran 25 May 1900

Bancroft

Lloyd D Grubbs 11 Jun 1900

William L Joiner 11 Sep 1901
James C Herford 13 Oct 1904
Hardy T Mysell 22 Jul 1905
Edward D Browning 10 Jan 1906
Gordy A Herford 19 Jan 1907
Asbury D Snider 8 Oct 1907

Johnsonville
Raoul Manuel 13 Jun 1900

Juanita
William I Vandenbosch 11 Jul 1900
Ben J Barrow 6 Jul 1903
Alfred J Burgess 19 Apr 1904

Perkins
Ivan A Perkins 3 Oct 1900
G H Ferguson 18 Apr 1904
Joseph Perkins 8 Aug 1911

Bonami
Burton H Smith 23 Jan 1901
Warren L Pickett 21 Aug 1907

Craft
Giels F Craft 26 Jan 1901

Lupton
Daniel P Lyles 30 Jan 1901

Cleveland[32]
Harry S Bridges 21 Aug 1888

Pickett
Christianna L Pickett 2 Aug 1889

Breland
William G Breland 6 Sep 1890

Crown Point
James Ellis 6 Sep 1890
Ivan A Perkins 21 Mar 1891

---

[32] Disc 18 Nov 1889

23

Mary S Escoubis 7 Nov 1893

Raymond
>Henry M Brown 27 Jun 1891

Johnson
>William C Johnson 13 Jul 1891

Silverwood
>Giles M Wing 4 Feb 1901
>J D Matthews 18 Jan 1902
>Sarah A Edgar 5 Jul 1906

Kipling
>William N Stracener 26 Jan 1901

Katydid
>Aaron P Crosand 13 Feb 1901
>Daniel N Moseley 25 Jul 1902

Coles
>John A Bush 27 Feb 1901

Rice
>Willis M Morris 31 Mar 1901

Rogersville
>Frances Rogers 30 Mar 1901

Joplin
>O B Scroggins 22 Apr 1901
>J L Doiran 11 Dec 1901
>Edward Morris 26 Apr 1902

Evins
>Willis M Daniel 22 Apr 1904

Florence
>J E Butler 11 Sep 1901

Orion
>Virginia Lanier 26 Apr 1902
>Willis Henderson 10 Apr 1903

Manchester
> Lea Paradis 13 Jun 1902
> Nellie A Marshall 3 Oct 1906

Rowson
> Herbert E Post 12 Jul 1902

Chopique
> George W Lacy 18 Sep 1902

Hewitt
> Thomas N Hewitt 22 Oct 1902
> Matthew Buhler 21 Jul 1914

Carson
> Mamie J Albright 10 Nov 1902
> Emma McKennit 11 Nov 1904
> Ernest E Fairbanks 23 Oct 1906
> James Crawford 8 Feb 1911
> Edna L Bolt 24 Jun 1912

Wasey
> William H Tolman 8 Jul 1903

Hecker
> Adeline Hebert 17 Apr 1903
> Raymond Hebert 26 Sep 1904
> John Hay 9 Dec 1908
> Fred Hebert 30 Sep 1911

April
> Green B Hennigan 5 Jun 1903
> John P McWilliam 18 May 1906
> Mary M Meadows 14 Feb 1908

Hayes
> Solomon Hayes 3 Oct 1903
> Felix Hebert 20 Mar 1911
> Walter Ivan Burleson 14 Feb 1914
> James L Thom 30 Jun 1921

Bell City
> Isaac Doiran 26 Oct 1904
> Gilbert Fontenot 20 Sep 1923
> Ferdinand Nunex 27 Apr 1925

Thornwell
      Jedean L Doiran 10 Mar 1905

Ludington
      Frederick W Hornibrook 16 Mar 1905
      Andrew J Lewis 7 Nov 1906
      Isaac Stephenson Jr 20 Nov 1908
      Dallas W King 1 May 1913

Blewett
      Robert C Adams 13 May 1905
      Andrew J Lewis 7 Nov 1906

Medora
      F M Strother 26 Apr 1905

Topsy
      B M Ball 26 Apr 1905

Rena
      William E Cole 24 Jan 1906

Woodlawn
      Dock Witherwax 26 May 1906

Fanistock
      Edward A Klock 1 Jun 1906

Newlin
      William G Strange 20 Jun 1906
      Leonidas Farque 1 Mar 1910

Ward
      Frederick A Rice 26 Nov 1906
      Cecil Smith 12 Aug 1907
      John L Ward Jr 1 Oct 1908
      Charles E Purifoy 12 Apr 1909

Longville
      Charles W Lawrence 4 Dec 1906
      Robert Jamison 20 Aug 1907
      William A Bohnert 8 Apr 1910
      Robert Jamison 5 Jan 1911
      William C Stewart 21 Oct 1912

Brimstone

Lettie Moss 26 Dec 1906

Elizabeth

Robert C Adams 3 May 1907
John E Smith 22 Oct 1908
Percy M Perkins 20 Sep 1909

Evert

Joseph W Barrow 18 Jun 1907
Milton E Howland 30 Nov 1908
George W Barrow 29 May 1911
Andrew D Lambert 27 Apr 1912
Lee R Lambert 10 Jan 1914

Reeves

David C Creel 13 Aug 1907
Joseph Iles 5 Apr 1913
David Cole 27 Feb 1926

Fulton

Stafford Cole 6 Jun 1908
Stephen E Stine 11 May 1912
Samuel McConathy 10 Aug 1913

Edna

Milton D Chitwood 21 Aug 1908

Bannister

Hugh B Curry 16 Aug 1910

Buhler

Ivy M Causey 12 Dec 1911
John H Pennington 22 Jun 1912
John F Faiszt 15 Nov 1916
Elmer Faiszt 18 May 1918

Coverdale

Benjamin Bertrand 7 Jan 1907

Creek

George A Perkins 14 Apr 1910

Moss Bluff

Reuben H Bomas 1 Jun 1912

Emad
> Maude Philyan 28 Jun 1913

Farwell
> Daniel D Blue 24 Oct 1911

Hutchinson
> Thomas N Hutchinson 20 Feb 1912

Ged
> Morris G Piercy 7 Mar 1911
> Tyra T Damon 1 Aug 1912
> Rosebud Potts 14 May 1922

Gola
> Whittle A Miles 13 Jul 1913

Grabow
> Daniel W McFatter 14 Jul 1911
> Cole H Wimberly 1 Mar 1913
> Fred Peninger 12 Jan 1914

Guy
> Edward E Richards 26 Jul 1909
> John I Lafleur 29 Sep 1911
> Bruce P Reed 21 Aug 1912
> Edward E Richards 2 May 1913

Hampton
> Edward L Williams 17 Jul 1912

Ikes
> Henry J Cockerham 24 Oct 1911

Newton
> Thomas F Burks 11 Aug 1913
> Sam Smart 13 Jan 1915
> Leroy Simmons 25 May 1920

Vizard
> Anthony Vizard Jr 29 Sep 1913

Lumita
> George Daglish 28 Nov 1919
> Arthur C P Tyler 9 May 1920

Gene

Lillie A DesJardins 5 May 1920

POST OFFICE	POSTMASTER AND
LOCATIONS	APPOINTMENT DATES

CATAHOULA PARISH, LOUISIANA

Aimwell[33]

M H Thompson 9 Jan 1873
Stephen S Ford 2 Jul 1878
Reubin M Beasley 29 Apr 1887
Reubin M Beasley 22 Dec 1891
Alfred W Crawford 27 Aug 1897
Eddy O Wright 6 May 1899
Alva Wright 19 Sep 1916
Lucious O Wright 25 Sep 1918
Eddy O Wright 20 Oct 1926

Cades

Aladan Broussard 25 Jul 1881

Castor Sulphur Springs

Joseph J McQuatters 3 Mar 1875
George Jackson 14 Jun 1875
Joseph J McQuatters 19 Jul 1875
Robert S Slemons 11 Oct 1875
Commodore P Keith 16 Jun 1876
John M Kees 24 Mar 1884
Frank M Mills 25 Aug 1884

Davis

John Randolph Binow 5 Mar 1879
Thomas M Butler 8 Jul 1884
William V Taylor 10 Jul 1886
William V Taylor 10 Jul 1889

---

[33] Disc 11 May 1874
Reest 2 Jul 1878
Disc 20 Feb 1886
Reest 29 Jan 1887

Stephen H Brown 11 Jul 1898
Andrew J Blake 22 Aug 1898
William H Norman 2 Apr 1903
Lonnie A Dunn 29 Feb 1905

Eden[34]

Phineas Whatley 7 Jul 1873
William R Whatley 15 Feb 1882
Joseph W Whatley 3 Jan 1900

Enterprize

Patrick H Carter 7 Aug 1871
Henry G Baughman 15 Jul 1880
Patrick H Carter 10 Sep 1880
Patrick H Carter (no date recorded)
John T Parker 28 Jul 1894
Cecie L Henigan 11 Jan 1898
James M Carter 19 Jul 1901
James Stewart 1 Aug 1902
James W Smith 17 Nov 1906
W H Luttrick 12 May 1908
Anette Pittmon 10 Mar 1915
Cornelius E Luttrick 9 May 1925

Funny Louis[35]

Martha Cockerham 9 Apr 1867
James M Adair 20 Oct 1873
Edwin W Yancey 27 Mar 1874
Uriah T Whatley 22 Oct 1877
William V Taylor 15 May 1878
John S Paul 19 Mar 1880
Isaac R Adams 29 Aug 1881

Green's Creek[36]

Thomas E Richard 2 May 1872

Little Prairie[37]

Michael Beard 3 Jun 1872

---

[34]Disc 1 Apr 1874
  Reest 15 Feb 1882
[35]Disc 6 Feb 1878
  Reest 15 May 1878
[36] Disc 1 Apr 1874
[37] Disc 6 Apr 1874

Glade

Effie M Beard 9 Nov 1888
George W Beard 19 Jan 1895
Effie M Beard 7 Aug 1902
Walter E Beard 13 Dec 1912
Mike J Beard 7 Feb 1916
Carrie B Coney 19 Mar 1917
Walter E Beard 20 Dec 1922
William N Mount 24 Jul 1925

Harrisonburg

William E Robb 27 Jan 1873
James C White 22 Jan 1877
Edward Dosher 31 May 1877
John H Carter 29 Jul 1893
John H Carter 6 Jul 1897
John H Carter 1 Jan 1921 (Pres)
Jean C Jack 24 Aug 1921 (Pres & Sen)
George L Hackney 12 Nov 1922
James K Stone 26 Jan 1925
James K Stone 1 Jul 1927 (Pres & Sen)
Henry B Talliaferro 8 Sep 1927
Jesse L Beasley 26 May 1928 (Pres & Sen)

Jena

James Forsythe 19 Dec 1872
Harmon Browning 3 Sep 1874
Jacob H Ringgold 4 Jun 1877
William C Coleman 6 Aug 1887
Charles R W Brown 30 Aug 1888
Shep B Hanes 1 Nov 1889
Richard E Hodges 14 Apr 1908

Jonesville

William P Cherry 21 Oct 1881
William P Cherry 11 Sep 1883
William Cherry 30 Aug 1888
Joseph E Cherry 26 Feb 1895
Mrs Elizabeth M Baker 17 Jun 1896
Miss Eliza Wheat 11 Jun 1897
Mrs Eliza Wheat Gray 11 Feb 1898
William S Jones 24 Oct 1902
Edwin R Ford 30 Dec 1904
Edwin R Ford 1 Jan 1917 (Pres)
Edwin R Ford 16 Mar 1917 (Pres & Sen)

Edwin R Ford 17 Jan 1922 (Pres & Sen)
Edwin R Ford 18 Jan 1926 (Pres & Sen)
Edward R Ford 1 Feb 1930 (Pres & Sen)

Kirk's Ferry

Ransom Hall 26 Jun 1872
John D Usher 29 Jan 1878
Nathan Fass 3 Mar 1879
(Illegible entry)
Stephen N Sojourner 19 Dec 1887
F A Jones Jr 7 Nov 1890
Benjamin E Carter 13 Dec 1890
Warren W Gilbert 5 Dec 1891
Zachariah Jones 15 Nov 1893
J N Hootsel 7 Aug 1902
Angie F Powers 31 Dec 1903
Fannie B Owen 8 Mar 1904
Stewart Montgomery 26 Sep 1904
Samuel F Hiper 17 May 1905
Angie F Powers 19 Mar 1907
Homer W Foreman 15 Aug 1912
J C Hutchison 17 Dec 1915

Lavacca

Mary E Bannermann 26 Oct 1881
Mary E Bannermann 26 Oct 1887
James W Smith 4 Feb 1901
Charles M Smith 21 May 1906
Henry S Bennett 27 Sep 1906
Ernest Breihaupt 1 May 1907
Joseph W B Gilbert 21 Dec 1916

Leland[38]

James E Kipes 23 Jun 1879
Elizabeth P Smith 9 Jan 1882
Ann E Smith 23 Feb 1882
Edward F Keenan 4 Sep 1888
Pleasant L Miles 11 Mar 1890
Conrad Weilenman 29 Jan 1892
Robert Lee McKay 17 Aug 1917
Mary A Bailey 30 Dec 1924

---

[38] Disc 19 Jan 1883
Reest 4 Sep 1888

Manifest[39]

Joseph N Thomas 19 Jan 1874
Benjamin F Huffman Jr 1 Dec 1874
Francis W Taylor 21 Jan 1878
John W Heard 30 Jan 1878
William R Webb 12 Feb 1880
Marion C Blackman 14 Apr 1882
Joseph N Thomas 24 Jun 1883
John W Heard 25 Sep 1883
Ruben N Streagall 24 May 1888
Philip E Girlinghouse 15 May 1918
Lillie O Richardson 29 Oct 1918
Meda McMillin 11 May 1921
Virgie Pruddhomme 16 Feb 1927

Parnham[40]

James B Wiggington 29 Jan 1873
Howard J Moreland 18 Jun 1875
William B Bruce 5 May 1878
William F Miller 7 Apr 1879
Joseph E Montgomery 6 Jan 1882
Alonzo F Mardis 19 Dec 1882
William F Miller 26 May 1888
Stephen A Clark 22 Jun 1916
Florence K Montgomery 30 Oct 1920

Pisgah

Joseph N Thomas 20 Mar 1873

Prohibition

Marquis D L Andrews 29 Sep 1886

Rhinehart

S T Yancey 4 Aug 1881
Jonathan N Luce 31 May 1882
Langston Yancey 20 Mar 1886
Joseph E Griffin 3 Jul 1899
Samuel S Andrews 19 Feb 1902
Daisy Moseley 16 Jun 1910

---

[39] Disc 30 Jan 1888
  Reest 24 May 1888
[40] Disc 3 May 1875
  Reest 18 Jun 1875
  Disc 13 Nov 1876
  Reest 5 May 1878

Langston Yancey 31 August 1911

Rosefield
H C Parker 22 Apr 1873
(Illegible entry)
Robert W Flowers 1 Nov 1885
George C Sorrels 30 Dec 1899
Robert F McGuffie 6 Oct 1913
Wyatt M Whitehead 20 Mar 1915
Julie Whitehead 3 May 1928

Routon
Robert W Crews 28 Sep 1883
David B Scarborough 28 Jan 1898
John M Pritchard 31 May 1899

Security[41]
James Smith 20 Dec 1875
Charles J Montgomery 17 Jun 1878
James Cook Jr 24 Nov 1880
Benjamin Campbell 17 Jun 1881
Emanuel Livingston 4 Feb 1896
Whitlock Norment 16 May 1888
Sidney Norment 14 Dec 1892
Deborah Livingston 4 Feb 1896
Louis Wohl 13 Dec 1897
Joseph W Henderson 13 Jul 1903
George W Beard 25 Nov 1908
Ella M Mount 15 Jan 1916[42]
William H Mount 15 Jan 1916[43]
Earl H Montgomery 23 Jul 1918
Travis E Barber 3 Oct 1919
George S Cotton 20 Mar 1921
Myra H Griffin 14 Feb 1922
Walter E Beard 24 Feb 1922
Howard B Campbell 20 Feb 1926

Sicily Island
Miss Sallie Lovelace 26 Aug 1872
Mrs Sallie E Stone 4 Jan 1877

---

[41] Disc 15 Nov 1929
[42] Postmistress and Postmaster hired the same day
[43] Postmistress and Postmaster hired the same day

Mrs Lorence Florence Curry 3 Mar 1877
Richard H Harris 14 May 1877
Mrs Laura B Enright 12 May 1879
John G Kostmayer 15 Dec 1880
Amy L Peck 20 Feb 1883
John Higgins 4 Sep 1883
R E Holstein 11 Sep 1883
Mary L Holstein 30 Oct 1883
Elizabeth Smith 22 Apr 1884
Mary E Sheppard 22 Aug 1898
Ida W Ford 13 Feb 1903
James M Coan 29 May 1914
James M Coan 1 Apr 1924 (Pres & Sen)
James M Coan 5 Jan 1925 (Pres & Sen)
James M Coan 26 May 1928
Mary Coan 18 Feb 1931

Stafford Point[44]

David Stafford 16 Jul 1887
Emma Lovelace 19 Aug 1893
William Reynolds 2 Feb 1894
Oliver H Martin 20 Dec 1894
Joseph D Clark 29 Dec 1899
John D Peck 19 Feb 1902
Amy L Stafford 19 Feb 1907
Mary M Peck 22 Apr 1909
Stephen D Clark 29 May 1911
John S Blackmon 22 Jul 1912

Summerville[45]

Isaac R Adams 25 Apr 1891

Tooley's[46]

Matilda C Fusler 27 Mar 1894

Utility

Samuel L Dale 20 Aug 1876
William H Waters 7 May 1890
Isaac H Boatner 1 Oct 1892
Ernest Young 9 Feb 1901

---

[44] Disc 15 Dec 1916
[45] Disc 14 Jun 1916
[46] Disc 15 Jun 1916

Simmons[47]

    John W Simmons 7 May 1886

Jack

    Jackson E Cockerham 2 Aug 1888

Trinity

    Leopold Moritz 29 Jan 1873
    Bernard Moritz 17 Feb 1879
    John H McCabe 11 May 1883
    Emile Enete 6 Jun 1883
    Caspar H Fulgaar 31 Jul 1884
    Hugh Watson 14 Sep 1886
    Philip Crooks 9 Nov 1886
    Frank O Worster 22 May 1891
    Emma E Snyder 16 Mar 1892
    Thomas H Folgaar 7 Sep 1892
    Rosa Snyder 24 Jan 1896

White Sulphur Springs
    George W Bethard 6 Apr 1880
    Mrs Sallie E Lovelace 15 Nov 1872
    William W Spence 10 Feb 1879
    John Enright 29 Jul 1886
    Mary A V Bethard 12 Nov 1887
    Brazzie D Whatley 2 Mar 1902

Wildwood[48]
    Frank J Bowman 26 Jul 1872
    Henrietta E Bowman 17 Jan 1877
    Charles O Bowman 16 Feb 1888
    Henrietta E Bowman 22 Jan 1891
    Mary E Bowman 7 Apr 1891
    Anabel R Bowman 19 Feb 1920

Tullos

    Cornelius G Dempsey 7 May 1891
    James G Holmes 11 Jun 1892
    William W Adams 13 Apr 1894
    William McDonald 19 Apr 1900
    George P Tullos 16 Jan 1902

---

[47] Disc 10 Jun 1887
[48] Disc 31 Dec 1920

Philip S Gaharan 15 Aug 1905
William W Adams 19 Mar 1907

Olla

William H Mills 28 Jan 1892
James H Babcock 27 Dec 1897
Isaac R Adams 23 Mar 1900

Rodgers[49]

Joseph Grice 28 Jan 1893
Jay W Meek 10 Dec 1896
George B Norris 9 Feb 1901
Henry E Machen 8 May 1906
J T Mitchell 7 Nov 1906
Robert Norris 18 Mar 1907

Peck[50]

Elizabeth Smith 2 Jun 1893
Horace Bondurant Jr 3 Jul 1893
James F Kiper 27 Aug 1897
Sallie Gaulden 12 Jan 1898
John W Cochran 22 May 1900
Robert L Jackson 8 Feb 1902
Bill H Hobgood 28 Nov 1903
Richard B Foreman 12 Apr 1918
Dan Kennerly 1 May 1918
Ralph L Matthews 15 Mar 1920
Walter S Knotts 17 Dec 1921

Nebo

John M Wilson 2 Oct 1893
James M Wright 9 Apr 1907
Martha B Bradford 11 May 1909
James M Wright 1 Sep 1909
Harvey I Brian 3 Feb 1910
John R Taylor 15 Nov 1910

Olympiac[51]

Mrs Matie G Brince 23 Jun 1894

---

[49] Disc 15 May 1903
[50] Disc 15 May 1927
[51] Disc 15 Nov 1894

Hoehn[52]
John Egloff 25 Apr 1895

Joy[53]
Edward Doughty 14 Aug 1895

Urania
Henry E Hardtner 30 Dec 1896

Gaulden[54]
Sallie Gaulden 29 Oct 1898

Maitland
Mrs Letty B Gillespie 17 May 1899

Nickel
John E Westbrooks 9 Mar 1900
John E Crawford 29 Feb 1908

Foules
Thomas F Hall 22 Mar 1900
J E Johnson 8 Jan 1901
William A Higgins 20 Mar 1901
Watson S Finister 4 Apr 1904
John W Brasley 27 Apr 1905
Oliver M Martin 9 Jan 1907
Watson S Finister 20 Mar 1908
William E McGraw 21 Oct 1912
Lydia R McGraw 4 Dec 1924
Anabel R Bowman 16 Jul 1931

Chantilly[55]
T B Nugent 18 Apr 1900
Samuel D Bowman 21 May 1906
Alex W Hanks 20 Feb 1912

Sherwood[56]
Walter F Holton 29 Jan 1901
Nathaniel T Owens 10 Dec 1902

---

[52] Disc 21 Jul 1898
[53] Disc 21 Feb 1903
[54] Disc 28 Sep 1902
[55] Disc 15 Jun 1915
[56] Disc 30 Nov 1929

Barney O Owens 4 Sep 1904
Charles F Smith 1 Jun 1905
Kuther E Jones 17 Jan 1906
Albert J Ziegler 22 Apr 1911
Fannie Babcock 31 Jan 1929

Cruse

Frank Cruse 23 May 1901

Perrin

Napoleon P Perrin 9 Aug 1902

Tew

George Davis 15 Feb 1902

Lee Bayou

Ernest L Gillespie 14 Sep 1902
Charles R Gillespe 6 Aug 1903
Thomas W Gray 28 Feb 1905
Henry E Hoover 31 Oct 1906
William H Bowman 30 Jan 1917
Mary E Bowman 15 Nov 1923

Little Creek

Edward Houghty 1 Feb 1903

Argo[57]

George B Klink 14 Jul 1903
Flora E Head 3 Oct 1905
John M Book 9 Oct 1909
Charles B Book 14 Apr 1915
Ethel May Book 18 Apr 1918
Willis Thomas Hooter 3 Jul 1920

Richard[58]

James B Price 13 Oct 1903
Kitty M Hodges 31 May 1921

Standard[59]

Shelly E Blackmon 9 Jan 1904

---

[57] Disc 21 Dec 1926
[58] Disc 31 Aug 1931
[59] Disc 22 Aug 1907

David H Duncan 18 Dec 1905
Mrs Cleo P Blackmon 27 Dec 1906

Trout

Ned L Kiser 31 Oct 1919
Jacob W Carter 7 Mar 1905
Andrew J Curry 9 Oct 1909
Anna B Lambert 27 Jan 1916
Dan Tarver 14 Apr 1927
Albert J Zeagler 16 Apr 1929

McKenzie

Henry Booth 14 Jun 1906

Chickasaw

Elisha E Andrews 8 Aug 1906

Mayna

Thomas B Floyd 13 Sep 1906
James S Trisler 7 Jan 1908
Joseph M Trisler 13 Dec 1912
Jennie L Trisler 10 Feb 1930
Jennie L Trisler 9 May 1930

Good Pine

Walter W Beaty 18 Jun 1907
James W Brown 10 Sep 1909

Bannerman[60]

Stirling S Boatner 28 Feb 1911

Serena

Henry C Holland 3 Dec 1908
Marshall K Trisler 5 Jan 1910
Jamie E Trisler 12 Jan 1918
Isaac S Crouch 19 Mar 1926

Walters

William A Smith 28 Apr 1916
George P Price 5 Nov 1918
Etta F McDougals 6 May 1931

---

[60] Disc 15 Jan 1915

Archie
> Joseph W Gilbert 2 Feb 1921

Larto
> Martha McNichols 20 Nov 1928

Webb
> Eva S Sills 3 Dec 1925

Wallace Ridge
> Charles R Blackman 17 Sep 1930

Stark's Landing[61]
> Mrs A E Allen 15 Feb 1876

Gludo ?[62]
> Michael J Beard 22 Aug 1877
> (Illegible entry)
> Noah Reddick 31 May 1881
> Michael J Beard 22 Jun 1886
> Mrs Effie M Beard 19 Nov 1888

Troyville
> Robert B Walters 17 Jun 1878

---

[61] Disc 21 Feb 1877
[62] Disc 21 Apr 1879
Reest 5 Jun 1879

POST OFFICE
LOCATIONS

POSTMASTER AND
APPOINTMENT DATES

RAPIDES PARISH, LOUISIANA

Alexandria Courthouse
William Mills Jr 12 Mar 1873 (Pres & Sen)
Calcott F Burges 26 Feb 1874 (Pres & Sen)
John D Lacy 13 May 1875 (Pres)
John D Lacy 21 Jan 1878 (Pres & Sen)
Frank Connelly 15 Jan 1880 (Pres)
Jefferson W Gordon 24 Jan 1881 (Pres & Sen)
Thomas B French 2 Apr 1885 (Pres & Sen)
Edward J Barrett 21 Dec 1889 (Pres & Sen)
Jonas Rosenthal 12 Jan 1894
Bessie G Wells 12 Jan 1898 (Pres & Sen)
Robert P Hunter 10 Jan 1899 (Pres & Sen)
John W Miller 10 Jun 1903
John W Miller 18 Feb 1904 (Pres & Sen)
John T Chamley 2 Mar 1908 (Pres & Sen)
John T Chamley 3 Apr 1912 (Pres & Sen)
Jonas Rosenthal 3 Apr 1916 (Pres & Sen)
Sherman Cook 2 Mar 1922 (Pres & Sen)
Roy M Lisso 31 Aug 1923
Roy M Lisso 28 Jan 1924 (Pres & Sen)
Leo A Turregano 6 Nov 1925
Leo A Turregano 18 Dec 1925 (Pres & Sen)
Leo A Turregano 8 Mar 1930

Asher[63]
Archibald Smith 2 May 1890
Miss Rose Smith 6 Jul 1894

Babb's Bridge[64]
Henry A Biossat 1 Oct 1877
Isaac N Erwin 1 Feb 1894

[63] Disc 2 Aug 1918
[64] Disc 30 Apr 1904

Bennettsville[65]

    Theoda Bennett 28 Apr 1906

Boyce

    William M Simons 18 May 1883
    Emma J Wells 30 Dec 1897
    Robert M Jones 14 Mar 1900
    Carey E Blanchard 16 May 1901 (Pres & Sen)
    Rufus R Robinson 14 Mar 1911
    Jay W Pawson 22 Nov 1912 (Pres)
    Carey E Blanchard 6 May 1913 (Pres & Sen)
    James E Roy 13 Jan 1916 (Pres & Sen)
    James E Roy Jr 1 Jan 1918
    Florence A Stuckey 28 Jul 1919 (Pres & Sen)
    Florence A Wilcox 13 Jul 1920
    Jay T Boone 17 Jan 1922 (Pres & Sen)
    Jay T Boone 18 Jan 1926 (Pres & Sen)
    Jay T Boone 16 Dec 1930

Cheneyville

    Francis W Marshall 16 May 1871
    Norton Roberts 17 May 1875
    Miss Eunice Bailey 20 Aug 1877
    Eunice B Roberts 3 Mar 1880
    John S Butler 27 Feb 1904
    Lancelot M Kean 22 Aug 1906
    Charles Manning 13 Mar 1907
    Charles Manning 1 Jan 1913 (Pres & Sen)
    Charles Manning 21 Jul 1917 (Pres & Sen)
    Helen S Barstero 2 Aug 1921 (Pres & Sen)
    George W Barstero 11 Jul 1925
    John B Smith 18 Dec 1925 (Pres & Sen)
    Louis E Rutledge 5 Feb 1930
    John B Smith 20 Feb 1930 (Pres & Sen)
    Fannie G Smith 2 May 1930
    Stephen R Jackson 20 Dec 1930 (Pres & Sen)

Crane[66]

    Caroline C Roberts 24 Jul 1882
    Miss Iva H McKinney 23 Oct 1886
    Monroe S Trimbe 2 Jan 1895
    Mrs Alice A Trimble 26 Jul 1901

---

[65] Disc 3 Oct 1907
[66] Disc 28 Feb 1913

Daniel P Robert 1 Mar 1904
Elizabeth A Robert 17 Apr 1906
Howard Hunter 5 Jun 1909

Elmer

Charles M Shaw 15 May 1888
Thomas A Nixon 28 Dec 1893
Richard K Johnson 11 Mar 1905
Joseph H Gray 13 Oct 1908
Alice Howerton 17 Sep 1909
Henry W Howerton 15 May 1914
William J Garou 26 Sep 1917
Clayton B Swift 31 May 1927

Gum[67]

William Odum 14 Sep 1880
William R Hargrove 4 Dec 1883
Obey Johnson 11 Nov 1886
Solomon Strother 22 Jan 1893
Elisha Lambright 25 Oct 1905
Warren Perkins 20 May 1914

Hemphill

Bettie Owens 12 Sep 1890
Jesse E Collins 27 Feb 1891
Wayman C Cudd 28 Apr 1893
C Holton 17 Mar 1896
H Rudisell 29 Dec 1896
John H Morse 27 Aug 1897

Hineston

Moses Rosenthal 1 Jul 1873
Stephen D William 1 Apr 1878
Mrs Mary M Williams 12 Jan 1885
Joseph W Williams 12 Mar 1906
Louis V Kirkpatrick 14 May 1914
Lydia Kirkpatrick 1 Mar 1915
Henry D Welch 15 Mar 1920
Webster T Crawford 20 Sep 1920
William T Crawford 28 Sep 1922
Jesse L Morrison 18 Nov 1925
M Golman 9 Aug 1928

---

[67] Disc 30 Nov 1915

Holloway[68]
>
> Thomas C Barron 7 Sep 1887
> Rueben M Blount 3 May 1895
> William A Smith 3 May 1898
> James A Christian 12 May 1898
> John O Beaseman 29 Jan 1899
> John O Beaseman 19 Jan 1900
> Thomas C Barron 19 Feb 1901
> James I Barron 9 Aug 1915
> C W Barron 9 Apr 1928

Lamothe
>
> James C Cooper 11 Apr 1891
> Pleasant H Davidson 25 Apr 1895
> William H Davidson 6 May 1904

Lamouri's Bridge[69]
>
> Bernhardt Mayer 26 Jul 1876
> David S Ferris 11 Apr 1890
> Robert L Sanford 29 Oct 1894
> David Weinberg 21 Jun 1895

Leon Station
>
> Charles C Cleveland 3 Nov 1886
> Alice L Sorelle 18 Jul 1900
> Thomas L Bedsole 15 Oct 1902
> Ella Cleveland 20 Sep 1906
> Lottie Bedsole 7 Oct 1914
> Rosa B Rachall 7 Feb 1921
> Barney J Beebe 23 Dec 1922
> Asa Beebe 4 Oct 1930

Loyd[70]
>
> Thomas C Wheadon 21 Apr 1879
> Lindsey L Brown 24 May 1883
> G V Wilson 29 Sep 1884
> Morris Weinburg 21 Oct 1884
> Rebecca Williams 27 Feb 1894
> Coleman Greenwood 6 Apr 1899
> William H Lyles 29 Mar 1901
> Joseph H Berthelot 13 Oct 1913

---

[68] Disc 31 May 1928
[69] Disc 31 May 1909
[70] Disc 30 Sep 1914

Melder
> Felix Van Melder 21 Aug 1884
> Henry L Melder 16 Feb 1887
> Daniel B Horgan 7 Dec 1891
> Bernard R Smith 3 Dec 1898
> John Melder Jr 27 Nov 1903
> Willie G Gilbert 1 Jun 1906
> Benjamin Reid 16 Jan 1908
> Felix H Turish 18 Jun 1908
> Willie G Gilbert 3 Feb 1921
> Artie M Barton 9 Feb 1931
> Artie M Barton 17 Nov 1931

Millford[71]
> John Cordukes 22 Jul 1875
> Mrs R D Cordukes 19 Sep 1881
> James H Sorelle 27 Nov 1883
> (Illegibe entry)
> Cordelia Lyles 8 Jan 1891
> Malinda E Smith 10 Apr 1894
> John Cordukes 28 Mar 1895
> Lydia Deshazon 17 Jan 1897

Moorland[72]
> Charles C Weems 4 Apr 1882
> J Eugene Johnson 30 Apr 1883
> Bernard M Hayes 28 Jan 1886
> Thomas C Wheadon 12 Mar 1890
> Floretta Wheadon 20 Aug 1896
> Levi Lehman 2 May 1898
> Whitty S Miller 16 Aug 1901
> Maron S Titus 27 Oct 1908
> Evelyn Drewett 12 Aug 1909
> Laura H Jones 21 Dec 1911

Pineville
> Edward J Barrett 9 Jun 1871
> Mary A Barrett 3 Apr 1884
> Andrew Davis 27 Jul 1884
> Edith A Houston 20 Aug 1890
> Andrew David 14 Nov 1893
> Alice H Wood 24 Sep 1902

---

[71] Disc 30 Jun 1897
[72] Disc 15 Apr 1914

Mary E Lawrence 3 Dec 1902
George W Lee 5 Mar 1908
Louise M Gamewell 5 Aug 1908
Charles G Turner 1 Jun 1910
William E Kees 30 Sep 1911
William E Kees 1 Jan 1913 (Pres & Sen)
Mary E Hunter 6 May 1913
Mary E Hunter 21 Jul 1917 (Pres & Sen)
Mary E Hunter 17 Jan 1922 (Pres & Sen)
Mary E Hunter 18 Jan 1925 (Pres & Sen)
Mary E Hunter 1 Feb 1930 (Pres & Sen)

Poland[73]

Joseph T Hatch 27 Jul 1882
Henry M Rodgers 27 Apr 1894
Moses W Gates 17 Mar 1908
Joseph L McGraw 25 Sep 1913

Quadrate[74]

Joseph W Swann 17 Feb 1892

Rapides[75]

James T Dezendorf 15 Jul 1889
Hattie L Dezendorf 16 Jan 1897
David Mayer 9 May 1902
William E Morrow 9 Feb 1908
Rosina W Mayer 11 Aug 1910
Josephine Adams 16 Apr 1915
Lillie Fausett 12 Apr 1916

Ryland[76]

John E Ryland 2 Apr 1892
Eugena A Deloach 15 Dec 1893
R W White 7 Apr 1900

Weil

Simon Weil 3 Aug 1887
Josephine Weil 19 Feb 1902

---

[73] Disc 30 Jul 1927
[74] Disc 31 May 1914
[75] Disc 31 Oct 1916
[76] Disc 15 Jun 1900

Welchton

Louis V Mallett 21 Apr 1887
Adolph Hartiens 5 Jan 1892
Adolph Hartiens 4 Feb 1897
Adolph Hartiens 27 May 1902
Ida E Flynn 10 Apr 1906
Mary Spencer Hayworth 18 Dec 1907

Morris

William J Morris 28 Sep 1892
G A Roberts 25 Apr 1893
William J Morris 28 Sep 1893

Bismarck[77]

Benjamin H Randolph 13 Jun 1879
Jasper B Dous 30 Jun 1892

Glenmora

Frank B Calhoun 13 Jan 1893
Amelia H Evans 10 Apr 1893
Robert Besscoun 31 Jan 1898
Henry S Melder 28 Mar 1902
William J Orr 9 Aug 1902
Henry J Lawson 25 Apr 1907
Edward L Andries 11 Feb 1911
Edward L Andries 1 Oct 1914 (Pres)
Edward L Andries 22 Oct 1914 (Pres & Sen)
Hadley R Morris 12 Jan 1916
Susie Jones 15 Mar 1916 (Pres & Sen)
Susie Jones 4 Jun 1920
Edna Byrd 11 Dec 1924
Edna Byrd 30 Sep 1929 (Pres & en)

Forest Hill

Jasper B Dove 26 Jan 1893
James W Cook 9 Jan 1894
William H Dean 20 Sep 1898
Samuel E Nixon 15 Mar 1905
Daniel R Johnson 8 Aug 1907
Floyd Peninger 22 Sep 1913
Fred Peninger 29 May 1916
Henry O Ponder 21 Mar 1919
Fred W Bertschinger 19 Sep 1920

---

[77] Disc 25 Jan 1893

Parks W Sansin 3 Nov 1924

Woodworth

George A Roberts 24 Jun 1893
John C Fontaine 4 Feb 1897
Edwin Rand 8 Jul 1899
Robert Stack 10 Feb 1905
James Luker 10 Apr 1907
Tyre E Banks 22 May 1914
Jay H Kenneson 3 Aug 1916
Jay H Kenneson 1 Jan 1921 (Pres)
Nelle Landrum 30 Aug 1922 (Pres & Sen)
Nelle Landrum 1 Jan 1925 (Pres & Sen)
Nelle Landrum 6 Feb 1925 (Pres & Sen)
Noah Wise 1 Nov 1926 (Pres & Sen)
Noah Wise 28 Jan 1927 (Pres & Sen)
Noah Wise 20 Aug 1927

Oak Glen[78]

William R Eldred 20 Feb 1894

Zimmerman

Don Green Petty 19 Mar 1894
Edward W Zimmerman 1 Jun 1901

Flowerton[79]

Frank S Flower 24 May 1894
Francis Cassell 28 Jun 1897
Charles M Flower 28 Jun 1901

Buckeye

Frazar Scott 12 Jun 1894
Matthew Rider 28 Apr 1898
James Noone 8 Mar 1901
Thomas D Daniel 30 Jun 1915
Benjamin F Kees 20 May 1916
Ellen Reeves 6 Mar 1918
Elias Paul 30 Jun 1925
Theason T Noone 28 Sep 1925

Longleaf

Alexander B Spencer 1 Mar 1895

---

[78] Disc 3 Oct 1902
[79] Disc 30 Sep 1901

James Holoman 31 Mar 1902
Claudia Jones 30 May 1912
Claudia Jones 1 Jan 1921 (Pres & Sen)
Claudia Jones 14 Jun 1926 (Pes & Sen)
Claudia Jones 20 May 1930 (Pres & Sen)

Flatwoods

Benjamin F Pate 3 Oct 1895
William A Lawson 27 Mar 1903
Benjamin F Pate 8 Oct 1903
William H Braboy 25 Jun 1904

Echo

Gordon V Wilson 14 Sep 1894
Paul A Lacombe 25 Jul 1899
Mrs Aloneida LaCombe 8 Jan 1901
Thomas J Richardson 17 Dec 1902
John Tullos 29 Jan 1908
Eustis W Kehler 2 Apr 1914

Ball

James T Ball 7 Jan 1896
Albert S Davis 9 Oct 1908
Frank Daniels 11 Aug 1913
Willie Hammons 10 Mar 1920
Darley D Bomar 29 Dec 1920
Ernest D Nesom 11 Jan 1922 (Pres & Sen)
Other H Hastings 12 May 1925
Biscoe Anthony 16 Apr 1926
Clarence W Brown 13 Jan 1927

Quarry[80]

Thomas S Hays 18 May 1896
Rufus J Garrett 27 Aug 1897

Sycamore[81]

Lewis C Bass 30 Apr 1898
Clinton Harrison 3 Sep 1912

Meeker

Samuel F Meeker 19 Jun 1897
Frank G Drouet 23 Jul 1899

---

[80] Disc 27 Nov 1897
[81] Disc 30 Jun 1919

Frank G Drouet 27 Mar 1916
John L Meeker 21 Aug 1916

Paul[82]

Herman Randow 27 Mar 1909

Westport[83]

Dennis Perkins 10 Feb 1909

Carmel[84]

Jesse L Mercer 10 May 1914

Gardner

William J Savage 3 Jul 1914
James A DeShazor 5 Apr 1920

Libuse

Behns O Venosek 3 Apr 1915
Martin Cizek 15 Oct 1919
Charles E Voda 19 Dec 1921
Emil Tuma 24 Sep 1928

Miltonberg[85]

John T Powers Jr 15 Nov 1915
Claude W Tatum 11 Jul 1918
Frederick F Rogers 6 Apr 1920

Wood Glen

David C Johnson 15 Jul 1919

Deville

Mary J Hayes 8 Aug 1916
William Bradford 15 Mar 1919
Joseph M Milbanks 6 Dec 1920

Kolin

Frank E Bailey 4 Apr 1917
Joseph Tauber 3 Jan 1920
Margaret Tauber 31 May 1921
Louis Filepe 6 Mar 1923

---

[82] Disc 31 May 1914
[83] Disc 15 Apr 1918
[84] Disc 15 Feb 1915
[85] Disc 24 Jul 1924

Bessie Svebak 18 Nov 1924

Lacamp

    Effie Long 2 Jun 1920
    J Webster Merchant 12 Feb 1921
    Parks W Sansin 18 May 1923
    Emily E Miller 3 Nov 1924
    Mrs Denise Jones 9 Dec 1926

Sieper

    John H Crosby 10 Jun 1920
    Rinda Ella Lloyd 29 Jan 1921

Tattoo[86]

    Henry J Melder 20 Apr 1922

Calcasieu

    David W Base 4 May 1925
    Elisha Brooks 15 Jul 1930

Otis

    Nannie Cranford 18 Jul 1910
    John W Cranford 13 Apr 1917
    Leo L Lankford 23 Jan 1920
    John H Coffman 20 May 1920
    Sallie M Arnold 8 May 1922

Koko[87]

    Malcolm D Frigdo 30 Jun 1917

Lamouri[88]

    David Weinberg 3 Jun 1902
    Daisy E Campbell 6 Mar 1908
    Daisy E Campbell 11 Nov 1911
    Annie E Dorsett 3 May 1912
    Gertrude Kerr 11 Mar 1914

Cornstalk[89]

    William Wiley 5 Nov 1909

---

[86] Disc 30 Nov 1927
[87] Disc 15 May 1918
[88] Disc 31 Dec 1914
[89] Disc 15 Oct 1910

Cloverdale[90]

> Sherman Cook 3 May 1902

Alfalfa[91]

> Gertrude Bowers 3 May 1912
> S E Bowers 16 Jun 1914
> Houston Wise 1 Apr 1927

Sherman[92]

> Henry Henderson 4 Sep 1902

McNutt[93]

> Webb Smith 6 Feb 1907
> Frank Gudenrath 24 Sep 1908
> Oscar M Hunter 14 Jan 1909

Meade[94]

> F O Hudson 26 Jul 1903
> William G Ratcliff 19 Apr 1904

Barron

> George C Barron 16 Jun 1912
> Richard J Sasser 26 Jan 1926
> Luther M Sasser 17 May 1926
> Joe Barron 12 Feb 1931
> James D Barron 26 May 1931

Clover[95]

> James M Marler 16 May 1904

Whittington[96]

> Littleton P Whittington 19 May 1905

Sharp[97]

> John Sharp 12 Jun 1907
> Amos Beebe 21 Mar 1911
> Amelia M Sharp 3 Dec 1914

---

[90] Disc 15 Oct 1910
[91] Disc 15 1927
[92] Disc 14 Sep 1907
[93] Disc 30 Sep 1912
[94] Disc 15 Mar 1913
[95] Disc 15 Jun 1909
[96] Disc 28 Feb 1918
[97] Disc 30 Oct 1928

Baxter K Sharp 12 Jul 1917
D R Strickland 30 Oct 1918
William L Lutrell 6 Sep 1919

Lecompte
Daniel G Arden 11 May 1893
Bodine C Peterson 12 May 1897
Sihla B Brown 15 May 1923
Sihla B Brown 7 Jan 1924 (Pres & Sen)
Sihla B Brown 13 Jan 1928 (Pres & Sen)
William L Brown 16 May 1929

Blanche[98]
William B Spencer 21 Apr 1898
Robert B Loveland 13 Mar 1899
Amelia H Evans 11 Apr 1901

Galbraith
Marine A Wright 1 Jan 1900
William T Massey 10 Nov 1908

Location Not Shown
Glover P Valley 10 Oct 1923
John H McCraney 29 Sep 1924
Robert J Merrel 30 Apr 1926
Archie Walker 8 Oct 1927

Quantico[99]
Levi Wells 15 Jan 1873

Spring Creek[100]
Lewis Q Barnidge 13 Oct 1871

Sullivan's Landing
John H Sullivan 19 May 1873
Rodin C Peterson 2 Feb 1874

---

[98] Disc 14 Feb 1901
Reest 11 Apr 1991
Disc 31 May 1908
[99] Disc 7 Jul 1874
[100] Disc 25 Aug 1875

Wellswood[101]

    Edward L Watkins 23 Jan 1873
    Montfort Wells 16 Nov 1874
    John R Grogan 22 Aug 1877

Kanomie

    Reuben H Carnal 2 Dec 1874
    Whitmet P Norfleet 6 Aug 1875
    Bernard D Meyer 6 May 1878

Bertrand

    William J Koehn 2 Jun 1874
    Miss Fanny C Smith 21 May 1875
    Mrs Fanny C Stevens 8 Jun 1875
    Lewis Richardson 24 Feb 1876
    Thomas P Dakin 23 Mar 1876
    Lewis Richardson 22 Sep 1876
    Jordan Gibson 7 Mar 1877
    Henry A Biossat 3 Dec 1877
    Jordan Gibson 2 Sep 1878
    Arthur C Watson 24 Sep 1878
    M M Marner 3 Mar 1879

Lecompte[102]

    Kenneth M Clark 21 Jun 1878
    S Bluestein 30 Aug 1880
    Joseph H Meeker 27 Jun 1881
    J R Williams 8 Jul 1881
    Benjamin Pressburg 6 Dec 1883
    Miss Bessie G Wells 16 Nov 1889

Booneville[103]

    Augustus D Harard 27 Jul 1878
    John T Rhodes 4 Nov 1879

Bayou Rapides[104]

    Daniel D Arden 19 May 1879

---

[101] Disc 4 May 1876
    Reest 22 Aug 1877
    Disc 11 Jan 1878
[102] Disc 5 May 1880
    Reest 30 Aug 1880
[103] Disc 27 Sep 1881
[104] Disc 16 Jan 1880

Cotile

     Hyman Bath 3 Mar 1873
     Joseph Malachowsky 18 Sep 1873
     Francis B Amsden 10 Mar 1875
     Mary Amsden 28 Nov 1879
     Rufus R Robinson 3 Jan 1882
     William H Simons 14 Jul 1882

Big Creek[105]

     Lavenia Jane Lovell 13 Nov 1871
     Lavenia Jane Lovell 27 Oct 1873

Mora

     Joseph S Kinglsey 28 Nov 1887
     W L George 27 Sep 1888

Dyer

     William Dyer Sr 13 Jun 1889
     John A Dixon 24 Apr 1890
     William Winegeart 17 Dec 1890

Midway[106]

     Mayo S Duke 31 Mar 1879

Westport[107]

     John A Hamilton 27 Sep 1881
     Robert Sweat 29 Jan 1882

Pacific[108]

     David A Smith 7 Sep 1882
     Henry A Biossat 22 Sep 1882

Levin

     Anger Siess 2 Apr 1892

Godwin

     William R Eldred 9 Nov 1885

---

[105] Disc 10 Oct 1873
    Reest 27 Oct 1873
[106] Disc 2 Mar 1880
[107] Disc 25 Jun 1883
[108] Disc 29 Dec 1892

POST OFFICE LOCATIONS	POSTMASTER AND APPOINTMENT DATES

VERNON PARISH,LOUISIANA

Almadane
>Daniel R Wright 3 May 1882
>John C Knight 19 May 1886
>James M Oakes 23 Sep 1896
>John C Knight 24 Mar 1898
>Beulah Knight 28 Dec 1903
>Samuel G Allardyce 8 May 1905
>Beulah Allardyce 20 Jun 1914
>Samuel G Allardyce 28 Nov 1916

Anacoco
>John J Kirk 28 Sep 1875
>Emma F Kirk 12 Feb 1894
>Thomas Mitchell 15 Jun 1895
>John K Foster 15 Jan 1896
>Letha Foster 21 Oct 1911
>John K Foster 15 May 1914
>Mary Stokes 20 Nov 1928
>Willie C Dixon 16 Nov 1931

Burr's Ferry[109]
>John M Liles 1 Jul 1873
>Charles B Burr 24 Apr 1876
>James C Roberts 13 Feb 1879
>John M Liles 18 Dec 1882
>Lewis A Perkins 14 Oct 1884
>James C Roebuck 15 Jul 1886
>Thomas C Wingate 24 Oct 1889
>James C Cavanaugh 5 Mar 1892
>Lafayette Jackson 28 Dec 1893
>Henry B Liles 2 May 1897

---

[109] Disc 30 Nov 1918

J B Evans 3 May 1898
Gilman B Evans 31 May 1898
Henry A Evans 23 Oct 1902
Robert D Cain 3 Dec 1902
John B Cluney 2 Jul 1912
Luther G Evans 22 Jan 1918

Caney

Thomas Richardson 22 Jun 1880
Patrick H Cluney 2 May 1898
John C Cluney 20 Jun 1914
Elmer S Bush 27 Nov 1929

Carmel[110]

Aplin E Chitty 13 Sep 1881

Conrad[111]

Napoleon B Johnson 19 Mar 1892
John Hunt 20 Dec 1897

Cora

Michael Smith 17 Dec 1887
Catherine V Boyd 9 Jul 1895
Andy J Boyd 25 Oct 1895
William J McDonald 29 Jul 1898
Elijah J Boyd 25 Oct 1898
Albert H Davis 29 May 1900
B P Braddy 28 Dec 1901
Andrew J Boyd 20 Jun 1914
Margaret M Boyd 26 Jan 1916
Jesse Boyd 17 Oct 1917
Jesse L Morrison 24 May 1918
Thomas Nessmith 27 Oct 1924
Hughes M Woodham 1 Jul 1927 (?)
J A Hughes 20 Nov 1928
Hattie Woodham 20 Nov 1929

Cottonwood[112]

Isaac W Midkiff 5 Jun 1891
Calvin H David 17 Oct 1905
Mary M Midkiff 11 Dec 1907

---

[110] Disc 2 Feb 1882
[111] Disc 27 Apr 1898
[112] Disc 30 Jun 1914

Mary M Midkiff 2 Sep 1908
Florence C Midkiff 22 May 1912
Auda Flora Midkiff 7 Jul 1914

Davis Mills[113]
John C Davis 10 Apr 1888
William E Fletcher 27 Dec 1897

Dido
John J Weldon 14 Jul 1886
John F Sirmons 2 Dec 1889
James E Sigler 15 Jan 1900
James D Stalsby 28 Dec 1901
John M Temu 11 Apr 1907
Robert A Reed 18 Sep 1907
Robert A Reed 7 Jul 1908
John F Belvin 24 Jun 1909
Charlie E Gibson 18 Jan 1912
John M Terrell 16 May 1912
William J Hall 4 Jun 1913

Elmwood
Nathaniel S Williams 26 Mar 1880
William D Williams 29 May 1899
Richard C Bierden 8 Jul 1901
James J Craft 23 Oct 1902
Edwin E Jordan 15 May 1914
Alfred D Foshee 3 Dec 1915
Richard C Bierden 15 Nov 1916
James C Cryer 15 Apr 1919
Elizer J Blackmon 16 Nov 1920

Hardshell[114]
Christopher C Hunt 10 Mar 1884
James W Brumfield 15 Mar 1886
Daniel R Gandy 29 Dec 1908

Hicks
James J Hicks 18 May 1887
John M Newman 11 Jul 1887
Daniel Johnson 4 Aug 1888
Charles Lewis 18 Jan 1895

---

[113] Disc 10 May 1898
[114] Disc 31 Oct 1918

Mrs Ada H Baker 2 Jan 1902
John M Newman 25 Oct 1904
Jesse H Cooper 1 Apr 1921
Joseph K Davis 8 Jun 1922
Nena Deason 2 Sep 1922
Edward J Jeane 23 Sep 1927
John R Mayo 20 Nov 1929

Leesville
Isaac O Winfree 22 Aug 1873
Cora A Bolgiano 20 Nov 1889
James Durham 20 Jul 1899
James Durham 29 Jan 1901
Edward L Wells 15 Jan 1902 (Pres & Sen)
Edward L Wells 14 Jul 1903
Jessie B Willis 18 Feb 1904 (Pres & Sen)
Jessie B Willis 14 May 1908 (Pres & Sen)
Benjamin F Conley 28 Feb 1910 (Pres & Sen)
Ada A Smart 3 Mar 1914 (Pres & Sen)
A G Winfree 28 Jan 1917 (Pres & Sen)
Benjamin F Conley 14 Feb 1922 (Pres & Sen)
Benjamin F Conley 23 Feb 1926 (Pres & Sen)
Benjamin F Conley 20 May 1930 (Pres & Sen)

Simpson
William A Jackson 29 Apr 1891
Miles G Parker 21 Mar 1900
Wesley A Jackson 4 Jan 1901
Frank D Jackson 4 Feb 1908
Robert L Jackson 20 Nov 1916
Archie D Jackson 31 May 1921
Cordia I Lewis 18 Mar 1925
Willie Smith 16 Mar 1929
Carl E Blackwell 12 Dec 1929

Slab Town[115]
James S Roberts 5 Nov 1887
John H Bedgood 23 Sep 1899
John H Bedgood 13 Dec 1899
Obedie L Bedgood 24 Apr 1906

---

[115] Disc 15 Mar 1909

Toledo[116]

      William R Shehan 26 Jan 1880
      John K Foster 31 May 1890
      Estelle R Ferguson 4 Feb 1896

Walnut Hill[117]

      Jessie E Collins 10 Nov 1873
      (Illegible entry)
      Samuel C Sweat 5 Dec 1879
      Samuel Roberts 19 Jan 1880
      Thomas H Bedsole 3 Sep 1885
      James G Hagan 20 Apr 1891
      John Ford 3 Mar 1892
      James S Derrough 29 Mar 1892
      John W Burns 21 Jan 1893
      Thomas S Franklin 15 Dec 1895
      Walker F Holton 24 Oct 1896
      William H Weeks 30 Dec 1897
      Robert J Dennis 19 Apr 1900
      Henry C Dennis 19 Apr 1903
      John W Johnson 24 Jun 1909
      William J Boyd Jr 11 Dec 1909
      Edward I Morrison 28 Sep 1910
      Daniel M Holton 21 Dec 1911
      James P Boneman Jr 11 Jan 1922
      Fannie M Parker 8 Apr 1925

Alliance[118]

      O N Davis 30 Sep 1898

Wingate[119]

      William F Craft 4 Jul 1896
      Edgar L Tuten 11 Jan 1900

Herbert

      John Lannis 4 Feb 1897

Hornbeck

      David B Pate 8 May 1897

---

[116] Disc 8 Mar 1901
[117] Disc 13 Oct 1879
    Reest 5 Dec 1879
    Disc 15 Nov 1925
[118] Disc 31 Jan 1899
[119] Disc 7 Feb 1903

Walter E Cary 9 Aug 1897
Sallie A Harrell 23 Sep 1914

Cooper[120]

Charles B Lockwood 2 Mar 1898
John S Jordan 11 Sep 1900
James W Oakes 21 Mar 1903
Elias P Franklin 25 Apr 1903
James E Jordan 14 Jul 1904
Cader C Miller 30 Apr 1909
John S Daniel 13 Jun 1913
Thomas B Smith 15 May 1914

Neame

Thomas H Walton 14 Mar 1898
William D McCalet 30 Dec 1899
William H Ross 31 Mar 1900
Abraham J Eichelberger 22 Jul 1901
Joseph M Nation 10 Sep 1901
Phillip J Schempp 10 Jan 1906
Catherine D Griswold 10 Dec 1919
Grace M Trusty 18 Jun 1913
Grace M Young 5 Sep 1914
Maud K Hayes 19 Sep 1917
Tucker Baker 10 Oct 1919
Clennie Craft 3 Mar 1925
Beatrice Parrott 5 Feb 1926

Rosepine

Thomas J Williams 6 Apr 1898
Henry J Fletcher 17 Jul 1902
Thomas Allen 12 Mar 1903
Henry J Fletcher 18 Jan 1904
Elisha J Sumrall 22 Aug 1904

Orange[121]

John P Cain 7 Sep 1898
Luticia Cain 23 Oct 1902
William C Downs 15 May 1907
Miss Letha Foster 27 Sep 1907

---

[120] Disc 31 Jul 1915
[121] Disc 21 Oct 1911

Hawthorne

James M Pate 7 Sep 1898
James M Killen 17 Jul 1899
Nathan H Bray 22 Sep 1902
William G Strange 17 Feb 1903
Thomas P Whitehead 17 Oct 1904
Robert W McClain 17 May 1907

Lake[122]

Edmond D Robertson 10 May 1899
Labie E Hitson 1 Dec 1915
Robert W McClain 16 Mar 1918
Cotie Lamberth 23 Dec 1922

Schley

Archie Farris 19 Jun 1899
James F Owens 24 Aug 1900
Fettick A Addison 13 Dec 1902
Nathaniel L Lee 7 Mar 1911
John J Newman 11 Jun 1914

Sea

William Taylor Smith 3 Jun 1899
Rufus A Smith 26 Apr 1907

Mayo

Elijah L Mayo 3 Jul 1899
William F Bryant 27 Nov 1905
Joseph O Mayo 25 Sep 1906
Elijah L Mayo 11 Dec 1907
Joseph O Mayo 5 Sep 1917
Napoleon B Mayo 27 Sep 1917
Elizabeth S Mayo 16 Dec 1925

Pickering

Edward C Pickering 19 Oct 1899
John E McFatter 13 Sep 1910
Carney Lee Brooks 23 Apr 1912
Philip J Schempp 11 Oct 1912
Thomas A Craft 5 Dec 1917
Ernest L Clough 27 Aug 1919
Thalia Feree 20 Nov 1923

---

[122] Disc 8 Apr 1905
(Illegible)

Niecie Rudd 29 May 1924
Jacob Winfrey 21 May 1926
Quintilla Clopland 2 Mar 1927
Quintilla Cleveland 13 Jan 1928

Everett[123]

Mrs Nancy F Everett 31 May 1900
James M Pate 16 May 1902
John K Foster Jr 1 Jun 1905
William H McGee 7 Nov 1906

Bolton[124]

James H Robertson 11 Jul 1900
Francis M Cooley 29 May 1901
James H Robertson 2 May 1902
William T Harville 25 Jul 1902

Sigler[125]

Eva E Duhon 29 Jul 1901
Nat Wasey 7 Feb 1902
Green W Foshee 24 Jun 1904
Ely Bedgood 12 Mar 1906

Hymers[126]

William Frisby 30 Jan 1901
G W Hymers 5 Mar 1901

Eddy[127]

Mrs Bettie A Faircloth 1 Jul 1901

Aubrey[128]

James B Stalsby 23 May 1902
Seth Martin 16 Jan 1903
Charles S Martin 7 Jun 1905
Rodolph Strother 10 Mar 1906

---

[123] Disc 15 Apr 1907
[124] Disc 15 Dec 1919
[125] Disc 7 Jan 1908
[126] Disc 15 May 1901
[127] Disc 31 Dec 1909
[128] Disc 11 Apr 1907

Hart[129]

    Wilber E Hart 1 Aug 1902
    William A Field 2 Feb 1904
    Calvin J Cochran 15 Apr 1909
    Laurence V Gibbs 11 Mar 1913

Drake[130]

    Martin V Johnson 25 Nov 1902

Barham

    James E Reeve 9 Dec 1902
    Walter B Gibbons 25 May 1903
    Henry E Stevens 22 Sep 1906
    Samuel K Turner 8 Mar 1909
    Jesse L McFatter 9 Feb 1914
    William C Sanders 3 Apr 1916
    Harry H Miller 15 Oct 1919
    Tina Dempsey 6 Oct 1920
    Lola J Hughes 6 Oct 1923

Bee

    James H Robertson 9 Feb 1903

Rudd Ferry[131]

    Alvin L Scoggins 20 Feb 1903

Leander

    James B McCullough 12 May 1903
    Leon W Smith 1 Mar 1905
    Michael Smith 29 Jan 1907
    Andrew M White 19 Jan 1915
    Nettie H White (No date)
    Jessie Catherine White 8 Jan 1921
    Ada Vashti White 9 Oct 1922
    Andrew M White 30 Dec 1926
    Isaac A Morrison 30 Oct 1928
    Andrew White 30 Aug 1929

---

[129] Disc 15 Oct 1914

[130] Disc 5 Jan 1904
[131] Disc 14 Dec 1903

Six Mile[132]

    Nancy E Harmon 14 Jul 1903
    James R Huggins 12 Jul 1904
    Clemie Hamons 25 Nov 1905

Sandy Creek[133]

    Henry M Calhoun 11 Jul 1904
    Young C Palmer 3 Nov 1886

Stille

    George W Boswell 3 Mar 1905
    Robert Edward Boswell 10 Nov 1920
    George T Boswell 19 Nov 1921
    Hattie M Burns 26 Apr 1924

Russell

    A C Evans 7 Jun 1905

Stables[134]

    Matthew F Myers 27 Jul 1905
    Herman M Graham 19 Apr 1906
    Joseph A Johnson 9 Sep 1908
    Hugh L McManus 2 Mar 1917

Auburn[135]

    George C Fort 8 Aug 1905
    Archey B Farris 16 Aug 1906
    Harvey B Windham 12 Sep 1907
    William M Ellis 22 Mar 1910

Redmond

    W R James 30 Oct 1906

Cravena[136]

    Frank G Price 15 Nov 1906
    Calvin Bay 23 May 1908
    Virgil L Millsaps 19 Dec 1910
    C Paul Leach 16 Dec 1913
    C Paul Leach 1 Jul 1920 (Pres)

---

[132] Disc 10 Feb 1908
[133] Disc 15 Mar 1905
[134] Disc 15 Oct 1917
[135] Disc 15 Jun 1915
[136] Disc 30 Jun 1928

Leslie M Hill 11 Jun 1921
Leslie M Hill 20 Dec 1921 (Pres & Sen)
Henry Johnson 14 Jul 1925
Henry Johnson 18 Dec 1925 (Pres & Sen)
Henry Johnson 1 Jul 1926
Henry Johnson 6 Aug 1926

Parkeville[137]

Samuel S Bedgood 29 Sep 1908

Fullerton

Theodore C Holton 9 Aug 1907
Bowman Marshall 2 Feb 1909
Thomas F Sheehan 20 Sep 1910
Thomas F Sheehan 1 Oct 1911
Thomas F Sheehan 18 Dec1911
Thomas F Sheehan 17 Dec 1914
Marion H Page 11 Feb 1920
Samuel S McCullough 10 Oct 1920
Marion H Page 12 Jun 1922 (Pres & Sen)
Marion H Page 14 Jun 1926

Nitram

John O'Quinn 23 Apr 1914

Farwell

Annie W Wade 13 Oct 1915

Liddy

Ely Bedgood 7 Jan 1908

Jewell

Emma A Ricks 18 Apr 1908

Nona [138]

James A Grant Sr 31 Jul 1909
John D Grant II 11 Oct 1917

Pitkin

Ely Bedgood 20 Apr 1908
William E Nolen 28 Sep 1911
F Holgan 19 Sep 1921

---

[137] Disc 15 Nov 1909
[138] Disc 15 Dec 1921

Simeon E Weldon 25 May 1923
Simeon E Weldon 1 Jul 1930
Leslie M Hill 22 Jan 1931 (Pres & Sen)

Whiskachitts[139]
William W Davis 12 Jun 1908

Daily[140]
Robert A Daily 15 May 1914

Dillow[141]
John B Gorum 15 Dec 1909

Essa[142]
Isaac N Addison 1 Jun 1915
Hester A Addison 16 Apr 1923
Mabel Nolan 20 Nov 1928

Evans
Robert D Evans 14 Apr 1909
William M Lofton 12 Jan 1916
James D Newman 10 May 1918
Thomas F Mitcham 6 Jun 1919
Katie Mitcham 5 Oct 1922

Hamons
Clemie Hamons 11 Aug 1916

Temple
Edgar Temple 23 May 1914

Pinewood
Benjamin E Poe 11 Sep 1912
Mims W Wimberly 28 May 1913
Henry C Brown 8 May 1915
Clinton E Allis 13 Mar 1916

Rena[143]
William E Cole 24 Jan 1906
Grover C Talbert 17 Jun 1914

---

[139] Disc 31 Jan 1909
[140] Disc 15 Jun 1915
[141] Disc 31 Jul 1911
[142] Disc 4 Mar 1930
[143] Disc 1 Apr 1916

Harley C Cole 19 Oct 1915

Tillman

Rodolph Strother 24 Apr 1911
Moses P Hale 1 Aug 1912
John W Stone 12 Oct 1914
John M Terrell 14 Apr 1915
Henry B Morrow 8 July 1921

Velma[144]

Hattie M McElveen 16 Mar 1910

New Llano

Walter H Freed 7 May 1919
William H Burton 4 Jun 1924
Robert B Snyder 15 Oct 1928
Clarence C Mickey 27 Nov 1929
John Aiton 26 Nov 1930
John Aiton 6 Feb 1930
John Aiton 1 Jul 1931

Slagle

Charles W Hidgens 4 Oct 1919
Charles W Hidgens 1 Apr 1921
Charles W Hidgens 22 Mar 1922
Miss Velsa G Hidgens 18 Dec 1925
Overton Smith 30 Apr 1929 (Pres & Sen)
Edna H White 1 Oct 1930

Belasco[145]

Benjamin F Williams 15 Oct 1919
William F Holmes 2 Aug 1921

Kurthwood[146]

Joseph H Kurth Jr 22 Dec 1919
Joseph H Kurth Jr 17 Jan 1922
Joseph H Kurth Jr 18 Jan 1926

Hutton

George Franklin Ross 19 Jun 1920
Samuel S Williams 11 Nov 1923

---

[144] Disc 31 May 1911
[145] Disc 30 Mar 1925
[146] Disc 1 May 1930

Claude B Graves 22 Oct 1924
Jasper L Surles 18 Jun 1926

Dusenberg[147]
Mrs Lawrence Currie 16 Nov 1920
William L Currie 12 Sep 1922
Claudia L Currie 24 Nov 1923
Claudia L Currie 1 Jan 1924 (Pres & Sen)
Claudia L Currie 1 May 1924 (Pres & Sen)
Mitch N Hadnot 7 Feb 1925
William J Lewis 8 Jan 1926
William J Lewis 25 Jan 1930

Lacamp
Denise Jones 9 Dec 1926

Knight
George W Hawthorn 8 Sep 1924

---

[147] Name changed to Alco

POST OFFICE　　　　　POSTMASTER AND
LOCATIONS　　　　　　APPOINTMENT DATES

WINN PARISH, LOUISIANA

Atlanta
> Mrs Emily E Peace 20 May 1873
> Mrs Addie Lecois 27 May 1881
> George C Lewis 28 Feb 1882
> George C Lewis 3 Apr 1882
> Mrs A Lewis 9 Mar 1883
> Mrs M Callie Thrasher 24 Feb 1896
> James Bird 27 Aug 1897
> Tom Pugh 3 May 1898
> Charles A Neal 31 Jul 1901
> Cornelia Ferguson 7 Jul 1902

Carthage[148]
> Edward Eagles Jr 15 Sep 1886
> Berrien Bailey 22 Jul 1898

Cold Water[149]
> Thomas E Thompson 7 Aug 1882
> Ambrose M Bryant 22 Oct 1883
> Delaney M Bryant 4 Feb 1896
> Jane R Williams 27 Aug 1897
> A L Martin 15 Oct 1902
> William Johnson 10 Oct 1905
> Ernest Leroy Taylor 14 Jul 1906
> George W Webb 25 Apr 1907
> Arthur Fort 16 Jul 1908

Conley[150]
> Charles J Phillips 3 Sep 1885

---

[148] Disc 18 Dec 1899
[149] Disc 15 Sep 1912
[150] Disc 30 Sep 1926

Nancy J Everett 29 Oct 1890

Flat Creek
  Samuel J Harper 3 Jul 1872
  George W Fletcher 12 Dec 1873
  William Fletcher 29 Jan 1874
  Hugh M Naughton 1 Jul 1874
  George W Fletcher Jr 5 Oct 1875
  William H McCarty 11 Sep 1916

Gansville[151]
  William M Moffett 20 Jan 1873
  James E Bain 21 Jun 1875
  George L Stinson 7 Apr 1879
  Mrs Lee J Wilkinson 10 Jul 1888
  Robert L Lewis 2 Jul 1895
  Joel D Puckett 26 Feb 1907

Hickory Valley[152]
  Amos M Casty 22 Jun 1874
  Samuel R Newsom 5 Feb 1894
  Mary Newsom 9 Mar 1915

Newport
  Levi Banks 3 Jun 1872
  William B Everett 18 Jun 1877
  John H Morris 28 May 1881
  Amos R Rentz 14 Dec 1894
  William E Chapman 21 Apr 1898
  Henry L McKaskle 3 Nov 1902
  Marian L Erskins 9 Oct 1903
  Thomas D Stuckey 27 Feb 1904
  Robert L Baxter 2 Oct 1906
  Hugh V Mayes 21 Dec 1910
  Mildred Wells 25 Jan 1922

---

[151] Disc 3 Mar 1875
  Reest 21 Jan 1875
  Disc 30 Sep 1911
[152] Disc 13 Apr 1929

Pine Ridge[153]

    James P Readheimer 23 Jun 1871
    John W Snelling 28 Sep 1875
    Smallwood D Clifton 20 Dec 1887
    Simma A Clifton 29 Aug 1888
    John D Meadows 23 Nov 1889
    George H Truscott 18 Jan 1895
    A J Clifton 16 Jul 1900
    George H Truscott 12 Jun 1903

Red Hill[154]

    James J Holmes 26 Aug 1887
    Abraham L Wright 12 Jan 1892
    John M Arledge 9 Dec 1902

St Maurice[155]

    Conrad Starks 12 Jun 1871
    William A Strong 11 Jan 1875
    H M Prothro 20 Nov 1877
    Jessie H Hickman 20 Aug 1878
    Mrs Sarah M Sims 10 Oct 1881
    Charles L Boulle 12 Jun 1882
    Henry T Carr 11 Nov 1884
    Elisha J Gamble 28 Jan 1886
    Benjamin R Allen 2 May 1895
    William M Teagle 1 Apr 1901
    Felix M McCain 17 Mar 1903
    Ludie D Jackson 28 May 1910
    Helen L Patton 8 Sep 1916
    Joseph C Nettle 8 Jun 1917
    Allie Jones 20 Feb 1918
    Elmo A Brian 15 Oct 1923
    Emira Jones 1 Oct 1930

Sills[156]

    Sarah E James 13 May 1881

---

[153] Disc 4 Aug 1874
    Reest 28 Sep 1875
    Disc 15 Oct 1918

[154] Disc 9 Sep 1905
[155] Disc 29 Oct 1874
    Reest 11 Jan 1875
[156] Disc 16 May 1916

James L Dark 17 Jun 1884
John M Jones 13 Dec 1886
Alexander P Collins 17 Jul 1890
Henry James 15 Dec 1895
Tennessee James 5 Mar 1901
John W Boyett 14 Mar 1903

Wattsville[157]
Delaney M Bryant 25 Jun 1889
James Carter 13 Jan 1891
Charles H Elliott 15 Dec 1895
John B Wilson 17 Jan 1901

Winfield
Austin C Banks 14 Mar 1872
J Meade Jennings 26 Apr 1875
David F Dunn 5 Mar 1883
Berrien Bailey 8 Sep 1900
Mary Belle Walder 25 Jul 1901
Lawrence E J Grisham 21 Jan 1903
Edward Eagles 27 Apr 1904
Edward Eagles 14 May 1908 (Pres & Sen)
Earl G Eagles 3 Sep 1912 (Pres)
George A Payne 20 May 1913 (Pres & Sen)
George A Payne 21 Jul 1917 (Pres & Sen)
Evandon M Chellette 14 Sep 1920
Victor L Brumfield 21 Jan 1922 (Pres & Sen)
William T Norman 14 Jul 1926
William T Norman 18 Jun 1930 (Pres & Sen)

Congo[158]
Carrie O Tison 16 Jan 1893
Andrew L Jones 27 Aug 1897
Ezekial B Powell 24 Mar 1898
Robert A Strickland 20 Jul 1901
J W Mathis 9 Oct 1903

Prairie Home[159]
William F Shumake 24 Aug 1893
John E Robinson 16 Nov 1893

---

[157] Disc 10 Apr 1902
[158] Disc 24 Dec 1903
[159] Disc 4 Apr 1907

Jeff W Hanchey 21 Aug 1894
George W Irvin 17 Feb 1900
Richard R Hightower 5 Mar 1903
Charles A White 17 Jun 1905
Andrew J Hall 29 Mar 1906

Zion[160]

James I Taylor 5 Feb 1894
James Cathey 28 Dec 1897
Nathan D Morris 4 Jul 1901
Houston S Morris 17 Nov 1904
Nathan D Morris 5 Feb 1906
Joseph W Peevy 30 Jul 1908

Payne[161]

Joel T Payne 19 Apr 1895

Grady[162]

Joel T Payne 25 Oct 1895
T C Kidd 16 Jan 1902

Cusetta[163]

Jesse L Wilkinson 16 May 1896
Adam B Anders 28 Apr 1898

Hill[164]

Henry J Perkins 10 Nov 1896
Allen C McCarty 18 Jul 1898
Daniel L Kirkland 12 Dec 1898
Iley M Erskins 9 Oct 1903
Alcy C Beavers 10 Oct 1904
James K Erskins 9 Apr 1917

Royal[165]

Ira James 17 Mar 1898
Mrs Ira James 3 Mar 1900
Thomas J Curry 30 Jun 1908

---

[160] Disc 18 Sep 1908
[161] Disc 21 Oct 1895
[162] Disc 16 May 1902
[163] Disc 10 Sep 1900
[164] Disc 31 Aug 1931
[165] Disc 15 Jan 1931

Curry[166]

> James C Curry 31 Mar 1898
> John T Odom 2 Jul 1914

Crockett[167]

> Francis M Walker 15 Dec 1898

Beech[168]

> Sarah A Smith 6 Feb 1900
> Hugh W Holmes Jr 1 Apr 1905

Mill[169]

> Emory A Golden 6 Feb 1900
> Joseph L Bewton 19 Apr 1904
> Emory A Golden 10 Feb 1905
> Joseph L Brewton 24 Dec 1908
> John L Brewton 18 Feb 1910
> Joseph L Brewton 14 Jul 1911
> Emory A Golden 12 Jul 1912

Dodson

> Adam B Anders 15 Sep 1900
> Felix T Walker 7 Jan 1902
> Joseph P Lucas 11 Jan 1903
> Joseph P Lucas 1 Jan 1921 (Pres)
> Joseph P Lucas 22 Sep 1922 (Pres & Sen)
> Joseph P Lucas 14 Dec 1926 (Pres & Sen)
> Joseph P Lucas 1 Jul 1931
> Joseph P Lucas 17 Nov 1931

Wheeling[170]

> Willie R Adams 30 Jul 1901
> John W Hughes 15 Oct 1902
> Willie R Adams 28 Jul 1905

Herschel[171]

> George W Burnum 30 Mar 1901
> R J Guthrie 2 Jul 1902

---

[166] Disc 15 Jun 1916

[167] Disc 15 Dec 1900
[168] Disc 31 Mar 1910
[169] Disc 11 Sep 1916
[170] Disc 21 Dec 1907
[171] Disc 3 Dec 1902

H M Johnson 9 Oct 1902

Tannehill[172]

    J Westly Boyett 14 Jan 1902
    George W Legan 23 Sep 1902
    James T Hall 5 Dec 1908
    John H Barnes 3 Oct 1911

Winona[173]

    John C Wepfer 22 Jan 1902

Sikes[174]

    William J Thornton 3 Mar 1902
    James W Sikes 8 Jan 1903
    Arnold L Sikes 13 Mar 1923
    Monroe Erskins 20 Sep 1924
    Monroe Erskins 1 Jul 1925 (Pres)
    Monroe Erskins 18 Dec 1925 (Pres & Sen)

Carter[175]

    Charles M C Martin 3 Jul 1902

Calvin

    Charles M C Martin 17 Oct 1902
    Carl A Robbins 5 Jan 1908
    Thomas J Brown 17 Aug 1908
    Carl A Robbins 12 Jun 1909
    George G Chandler 27 Jan 1914
    William J Bice 6 Jun 1916
    John T Bice 16 Jan 1920

Moore

    Thomas R Knight 23 Feb 1904
    Lamar L Melton 30 Dec 1904

Alonzo[176]

    Selestie K Smith 21 Mar 1904
    Benjamin F Barton 12 Nov 1904
    William L Whorton 24 Nov 1905

---

[172] Disc 3 Dec 1911
[173] Disc 15 Jan 1910
[174] Disc 29 Aug 1929
[175] Disc 17 Oct 1902
[176] Disc 25 Jan 1906

Lofton[177]

> William T Purvis 28 Apr 1904
> Eugenia Hall 30 Jan 1905
> John F Boze 30 Sep 1905
> Jackson T Payne 11 Jan 1906
> John F Boze 29 Jun 1907
> Hiram B Bradford 22 Nov 1907
> Thomas L Cooper 26 Feb 1912

Fay[178]

> Arthur Fort 29 Sep 1913

Smith[179]

> John L Lucas 6 Aug 1904

Fatama[180]

> William T Nelson 27 Oct 1904

Whitford[181]

> William Wepfer 2 Dec 1905
> James H Smith 1 Mar 1910

Salt[182]

> Mary F Boyd 13 Feb 1906

Emden[183]

> James E Drewett 7 Jul 1906
> Edward W Need 13 Mar 1908

Bogalusa

> M Babington 17 Jul 1906

Packton[184]

> Walter Slay 13 Sep 1907

Grace[185]

> John M Taylor 18 Jun 1907

---

[177] Disc 28 Feb 1918
[178] Disc 15 Sep 1917
[179] Disc 15 Dec 1911
[180] Disc 22 Oct 1907
[181] Disc 30 Nov 1913
[182] Disc 31 Dec 1909
[183] Disc 30 Oct 1909
[184] Disc 31 Mar 1928
[185] Disc 31 Dec 1918

Walter W McDowell 23 Dec 1907
Thomas H Mathis 16 Jan 1908
David F Corley 23 Apr 1909
Duke K Hayes 21 Feb 1911
George W McMillian 26 Apr 1913
Lillard Lowdermilk 20 Aug 1917
Arthur Fort 7 Jun 1918

Needmore[186]

Arthur B Branch 18 Jun 1909

Machen[187]

Henry E Machen 4 Sep 1907

Dugdemona[188]

Charles E Freed 14 Apr 1908

Oak[189]

James R Smith 24 Apr 1910

Wellsir[190]

Thomas M Thames 18 Sep 1905
Nola Shirley 18 Oct 1912

Banks[191]

Calvin W Spiegle 26 Aug 1911
Andrew J Crain 1 Oct 1912
Charles H Haynes 2 Dec 1913
Jesse McKaskle 23 Nov 1916

Chester[192]

Lee E Rogers 5 Apr 1910
Warren P Myers 17 May 1918

Crews[193]

William R Tilton 17 Jun 1914
Bessie F Jones 19 Jan 1916

---

[186] Disc 1 Apr 1911
[187] Disc 30 Sep 1911
[188] Disc 11 Jan 1909
[189] Disc 15 Nov 1911
[190] Disc 24 Jan 1914
[191] Disc 15 May 1918
[192] Disc 31 May 1920
[193] Disc 6 Nov 1926

Louise Boykin 7 Feb 1921
Hughey J Toliver 17 Apr 1922
Louise Boykin 17 May 1926

Hinton

Grady T Hinton 30 Jun 1910

Joyce

George H Griffith 17 May 1917
Peter H Michael 10 Jan 1918
Lora B Farris 27 May 1920
Eunice Gunn 13 Mar 1922
Eva Adams 3 Aug 1923
Myrtle K Long 21 Feb 1924
Gertrude Moore 21 Apr 1926
Mrs Zetta Wade 19 Jul 1926
Marie Parrish 2 Dec 1929
Marie Parrish 30 Jan 1930
Mrs R H Creek 30 Oct 1930
Leona Creel 19 Dec 1930

Index

Baker
    Alexander S, 2
    Fidello C, 13
    James J, 17
    Mrs Ada H, 61
    Mrs Elizabeth M, 32
    Robert H, 3
    Tucker, 63
Ball
    B M, 26
    James T, 51
Banks
    Austin C, 75
    Levi, 73
    Tyre E, 50
Bannermann
    Mary E, 33
Barbe
    Charvey, 15
Barber
    Travis E, 35
Barnard
    S A, 4
Barnes
    John H, 78
Barnidge
    Lewis Q, 55
Barrett
    Edward J, 43, 47
    Mary A, 47
Barron
    C W, 46
    George C, 54
    James D, 54
    James I, 46
    Joe, 54
    Thomas C, 46
Barrow
    Ben J, 23
    George W, 27
    Joseph W, 11, 27

Barstero
    George W, 44
    Helen S, 44
Barton
    Artie M, 47
    Benjamin F, 78
Base
    David W, 53
Bass
    Lewis C, 51
Batchelor
    Ernest D, 22
Bath
    Hyman, 57
Baughman
    Henry G, 31
Baxter
    Robert L, 73
Bay
    Calvin, 67
Beard
    Effie M, 32, 42
    George W, 32, 35
    James G, 20
    Michael, 31
    Michael J, 42
    Mike J, 32
    Walter E, 32, 35
Beaseman
    John O, 46
Beasley
    Jesse L, 32
    Reubin M, 30
Beaty
    Walter W, 41
Beavers
    Alcy C, 76
Bedgood
    Ely, 65, 68
    John H, 61
    Obedie L, 61
    Samuel S, 68

Bedsole
  Lottie, 46
  Thomas H, 62
  Thomas L, 46
Beebe
  Amos, 54
  Asa, 46
  Barney J, 46
Belvin
  John F, 60
Bennett
  Henry S, 33
  Theoda, 44
Bentley
  William J, 4
Berand
  Thomas L, 3
Berlin
  Hattie, 4
  Joseph A, 5
  Mary B, 5
  Nicholas J, 5
Bernard
  Stephen A, 8
Berthelot
  Joseph H, 46
Berthune
  Walter F, 16
Bertrand
  Benjamin, 27
Bertschinger
  Fred W, 49
Besscoun
  Robert, 49
Bethard
  George W, 37
  Mary A V, 37
Bettevy
  Miche, 7
Bewton
  Joseph L, 77
Bice

  John T, 78
  William J, 78
Bielkiewicz
  C, 4
  Henry, 4
Bierden
  Richard C, 60
Bihm
  Milton, 10
Binow
  John Randolph, 30
Biossat
  Henry A, 43, 56, 57
Bird
  James, 72
Biven
  Samuel, 13
Bize
  Jeanne, 6
Blackman
  Charles R, 42
  Marion C, 34
Blackmon
  Elizer J, 60
  John S, 36
  Mrs Cleo P, 41
  Shelly E, 40
Blackwell
  Carl E, 61
Blackwood
  Elder G, 5
  Eldred, 5
Blake
  Andrew J, 31
Blakewood
  Bettison W, 5
Blanchard
  Carey E, 44
Blount
  Rueben M, 46
Blue
  Daniel D, 28

John S, 44
Thomas M, 30
Byrd
  Edna, 49
Cain
  James O E, 4
  John P, 63
  Luticia, 63
  Robert D, 59
Calhoun
  Frank B, 49
  Henry M, 67
Callahan
  Lena, 4
Callegori
  Louis F, 2
  Serge, 2
Campbell
  Benjamin, 35
  Daisy E, 53
  Howard B, 35
Cannon
  Ethelbert L, 16
Cappel
  Calvin D, 3
  Joseph, 3
Car
  Benjamin F, 12
Carnal
  Reuben H, 56
Carpenter
  Louis W, 8
Carr
  Henry T, 74
Carruth
  Thomas J, 8, 9
Carter
  Benjamin E, 33
  Henry E, 13
  Jacob W, 41
  James, 75

James M, 31
John H, 32
Levi P, 1, 2
Patrick H, 31
Cary
  Mary C, 17
  Walter E, 63
Cassell
  Francis, 50
Casty
  Amos M, 73
Cathey
  James, 76
Causey
  Ivy M, 27
Cavanaugh
  James C, 58
Cazale
  Joseph P, 4
Chafin
  Winburn L, 8
Chamley
  John T, 43
Chandler
  George G, 78
Chapman
  William E, 73
Chauffepied
  John H, 2, 9
Chellette
  Evandon M, 75
Chenier
  Joseph, 10, 16, 17
Chenvert
  Maise E, 7
  Marcelina, 7
Cherry
  Joseph E, 32
  William, 32
  William P, 32
Chesson
  John C, 12

James C, 46
Jesse H, 61
Thomas L, 79
Coplen
James R, 18
Cordukes
John, 47
Mrs R D, 47
Corley
David F, 80
Cosand
Aaron P, 21
Cotton
George S, 35
Courmier
Jack, 22
Couvillion
Henry F, 7
Sambola L, 6
Couvillon
Eugene, 4
Lu J, 6
Olivier P, 5
Walter F, 4
Cox
Richard H, 7
Coyle
Walter F, 3
Craddock
Joseph C, 20
Craft
Clennie, 63
Giels F, 23
James J, 60
Thomas A, 64
William F, 62
Crain
Andrew J, 80
Cranford
John W, 53
Nannie, 53
Crawford

Alfred W, 30
James, 25
John E, 39
Webster T, 45
William T, 45
Creek
Mrs R H, 81
Creel
David C, 17, 27
Leona, 81
Crews
Robert W, 35
Crooks
Philip, 37
Crosand
Aaron P, 24
Crosby
John H, 53
Crouch
Isaac S, 41
Cruse
Frank, 40
Cryer
James C, 60
Cudd
Wayman C, 45
Currie
Claudia L, 71
Mrs Lawrence, 71
William L, 71
Curry
Andrew J, 41
Hugh B, 20, 27
James C, 77
Mrs Lorence Florence, 36
Thomas J, 76
Daglish
George, 28
Daily
Robert A, 69
Dakin
Thomas P, 56

Fletcher
George W, 73
Henry J, 63
William, 73
William E, 21, 60
Flower
Charles M, 50
Frank S, 50
Flowers
Robert W, 35
Floyd
Thomas B, 41
Flynn
Ida E, 49
Foley
Josey P, 4
Folgaar
Thomas H, 37
Fontaine
John C, 50
Fontenot
Gilbert, 25
Ford
Abbie, 18
Edward R, 33
Edwin R, 32, 33
George H, 12
Ida W, 36
John, 62
Stephen S, 30
Foreman
Homer W, 33
Richard B, 38
Forsythe
James, 32
Fort
Arthur, 72, 79, 80
George C, 67
Foshee
Alfred D, 60
Green W, 65
Foster

Dennis M, 15, 16
Harmon D, 22
John K, 58, 62, 65
Letha, 58, 63
Lucy L, 21
Franklin
Elias P, 63
Thomas S, 62
Frazar
Moses E, 16
Fredericks
John, 21
Freed
Charles E, 80
Walter H, 70
French
Thomas B, 43
Frigdo
Malcolm D, 53
Frisby
William, 65
Fulgaar
Caspar H, 37
Funk
Michael, 12
Fusler
Matilda C, 36
Gaharan
Philip S, 38
Gaidry
Octave, 17, 20
Gailbraith
Alice L, 21
Gamble
Elisha J, 74
Gamewell
Louise M, 48
Gammage
Ector R, 13, 18
Gandy
Daniel R, 60
Samuel A, 13

Garou
    William J, 45
Garrett
    J M, 13
    Rufus J, 51
Gaspard
    Josephine, 5
Gates
    Moses W, 48
Gaulden
    Sallie, 38, 39
Gauthier
    Emile, 2
    L L, 4
Geary
    Harry J, 16
    James P, 15
George
    W L, 57
Gibbons
    Walter B, 66
Gibbs
    Laurence V, 66
Gibson
    Charlie E, 60
    Jordan, 56
Gilbert
    Joseph W, 42
    Joseph W B, 33
    Warren W, 33
    Willie G, 47
Gill
    Hardy C, 11
Gillespe
    Charles R, 40
Gillespie
    Ernest L, 40
    Mrs Letty B, 39
Gillis
    Cyrus W, 20
Girlinghouse
    Philip E, 34

Golden
    Emory A, 77
Golman
    M, 45
Good
    Mrs Annie B, 13
Gordon
    Jefferson W, 43
    Walthall B, 7
    William C, 7
Gorman
    Clement W, 15
Gorum
    John B, 69
Goss
    George F, 14
Goudeau
    Ada E, 5
    Adolph A, 5
Graham
    Herman M, 67
Granger
    Frank, 18
Grant
    James A, 14
    James A, 14, 68
Grant II
    John D, 68
Graves
    Claude B, 71
Gray
    Joseph H, 45
    Mrs Eliza Wheat, 32
    Thomas W, 40
Greene
    Preston P, 22
Greenwood
    Coleman, 46
Gremillion
    F M, 7
    Gustave P, 5
    Leon B, 5

Grice
  Joseph, 38
Griffin
  James T, 1
  Joseph E, 34
  Mrs Effa S, 1
  Myra H, 35
Griffith
  George H, 81
  Isaac, 12
Grisham
  Lawrence E J, 75
Griswold
  Catherine D, 63
Grogan
  John R, 56
Grubbs
  Lloyd D, 22
Gudenrath
  Frank, 54
Gunn
  Eunice, 81
Guthrie
  R J, 77
Haas
  A Marshall, 3
  Alexander M, 8
Hackney
  George L, 32
Hadnot
  Mitch N, 71
Hagan
  James G, 62
Hale
  Moses P, 70
Hall
  Andrew J, 76
  Ashley B, 19
  Edward J, 15
  Eugenia, 79
  Henry E, 22
  Henry V, 14

  James T, 78
  Mrs Mary H, 6
  Ransom, 33
  Thomas F, 39
  William J, 60
Hamilton
  Corinne C, 4
  James I, 19
  John A, 57
  May, 19
Hammons
  Willie, 51
Hamons
  Clemie, 67, 69
Hanchey
  Jeff W, 76
Hanes
  Shep B, 32
Hanks
  Alex W, 39
Harard
  Augustus D, 56
Hardtner
  Henry E, 39
Hargrave
  William, 20
Hargrove
  William R, 45
Harmon
  Nancy E, 67
Harper
  Samuel J, 73
Harrell
  Sallie A, 63
Harris
  Richard H, 36
Harrison
  Clinton, 51
Hart
  Dan W, 5
  Wilber E, 66
Hartiens

Adolph, 49
Harville
  William T, 65
Haskell
  W H, 15
Hastings
  Other H, 51
Hatch
  Joseph T, 48
Hauck
  Edward L, 13
Haves
  John D, 20
Hawthorn
  George W, 71
Hay
  John, 25
Hayes
  Bernard M, 47
  Duke K, 80
  Eugene C, 3
  Mary J, 52
  Maud K, 63
  Solomon, 25
Haynes
  Charles H, 80
Hays
  Thomas S, 51
Hayworth
  Mary Spencer, 49
Head
  Flora E, 40
Heard
  George W, 10
  John W, 34
  Thomas J, 8
Hebert
  Adeline, 25
  Alexander P, 15
  Felix, 25
  Fred, 25
  Joseph D, 2

Pierre A, 15
  Raymond, 25
Heins
  Frank H, 21
Hellinger
  Joseph, 20
Henderson
  Henry, 54
  Henry D, 22
  Isaac M, 20
  Joseph W, 35
  Willis, 24
Henigan
  Cecie L, 31
Hennigan
  Gilbert F, 16
  Green B, 25
  James E M, 16
  John T, 18
Henning
  John T, 18
Herford
  Drew D, 21
  Estelle, 16
  Gordy A, 23
  J Lee, 22
  James C, 23
Herron
  William T, 22
Hetherwick
  Clarence, 7
  Jefferson, 7
Hewitt
  Eugene, 16
  Thomas N, 17, 25
Hickman
  Jessie H, 74
Hicks
  James J, 60
Hidgens
  Charles W, 70

Miss Velsa G, 70
Higgins
  Charles T, 13
  John, 36
  William A, 39
Hightower
  Richard R, 76
Hill
  John, 11
  Leslie M, 68, 69
Hillebrandt
  James, 18
Hinton
  Grady T, 81
Hiper
  Samuel F, 33
Hitson
  Labie E, 64
Hobgood
  Bill H, 38
Hodges
  Kitty M, 40
  Richard E, 32
Holbrook
  William A, 20
Holden
  Simon, 7
Holgan
  F, 68
Holland
  Henry C, 41
Holmes
  James G, 37
  James J, 74
  William F, 70
Holmes Jr
  Hugh W, 77
Holoman
  James, 51
Holstein
  Mary L, 36
  R E, 36

Holton
  C, 45, 68
  Daniel M, 62
  Walker F, 62
  Walter F, 39
Hooter
  Louis, 1
  Willis Thomas, 40
Hootsel
  J N, 33
Hoover
  Henry E, 40
Horgan
  Daniel B, 47
Hornibrook
  Frederick W, 26
Houghty
  Edward, 40
Houston
  Edith A, 47
Howard
  William R, 7
Howerton
  Alice, 45
  Henry W, 45
Howland
  Milton E, 27
Hudson
  Daniel B, 2, 3, 8, 9
  F O, 54
  George B, 3
  Mrs Laura F, 3, 9
Huesman
  Charles F, 6
Huffman Jr
  Benjamin F, 34
Huggins
  James R, 67
Hughes
  J A, 59
  John W, 77
  Lola J, 66

Joiner
  William L, 23
Jones
  Allie, 74
  Andrew L, 75
  Bessie F, 80
  Blance M, 20
  Claudia, 51
  Denise, 71
  Emira, 74
  John M, 75
  Kuther E, 40
  Laura H, 47
  Mrs Denise, 53
  Robert M, 44
  Susie, 49
  William S, 32
  Zachariah, 33
Jones Jr
  F A, 33
Jordan
  Edwin E, 60
  James E, 63
  John S, 63
Kean
  Lancelot M, 44
Keenan
  Edward F, 33
Kees
  Benjamin F, 50
  John M, 30
  William E, 48
Kehler
  Eustis W, 51
Keith
  Commodore P, 30
Kellis
  Harvey C, 20
Kennerly
  Dan, 38
Kenneson

Jay H, 50
Kent
  Joseph T, 10
  William T, 21
Kerr
  Gertrude, 53
Kidd
  T C, 76
Killen
  James M, 64
Kimbro
  Thomas B, 1
King
  Dallas W, 26
Kingery
  Catherine, 15
  Charles W, 15
  Joseph J, 17
  Samson R, 17
  Samuel R, 20
Kinglsey
  Joseph S, 57
Kiper
  James F, 38
Kipes
  James E, 33
Kirk
  Emma F, 58
  John J, 58
Kirkland
  Daniel L, 76
Kirkpatrick
  Louis V, 45
  Lydia, 45
Kirman
  J B, 15
Kiser
  Ned L, 41
Klink
  George B, 40
Klock
  Edward A, 26

Knight
    Beulah, 58
    Henry A, 11
    John C, 58
    Thomas R, 78
    Willie H, 22
Knotts
    Walter S, 38
Koehn
    William J, 56
Kurth Jr
    Joseph H, 70
Laborde
    Tempey, 9
LaComb
    Martin M, 2, 9
Lacombe
    Paul A, 51
LaCombe
    Mrs Aloneida, 51
Lacy
    George W, 25
    John D, 43
Lafargue
    Mrs Edwin L, 6
Lafleur
    A Phonlin, 4
    Ernest, 12
    John I, 28
    Joseph D, 17
    Paul W, 4
Lambert
    Andrew D, 27
    Anna B, 41
    Lee R, 27
Lamberth
    Cotie, 64
Lambright
    Elisha, 45
Landrum
    Nelle, 50
Langdon

    Perry L, 14
Langlaid
    Ozia, 4
Lanier
    Virginia, 24
Lankford
    Leo L, 53
Lannis
    John, 62
Lansdell
    Walter T, 3
Laurents
    Felix, 15
Lawrence
    Charles W, 26
    Mary E, 48
Lawson
    Henry J, 49
    William A, 51
Lawther
    James V, 9
    William, 9
Leach
    C Paul, 67
LeBlanc
    Felix L, 13
    Joseph M, 22
Lecois
    Mrs Addie, 72
Ledoux
    Ozette, 19
Lee
    George W, 48
    Maria Agnes, 15
    Nathaniel L, 64
Legan
    George W, 78
Lehman
    Levi, 47
Leigh
    Mrs Azema, 3
Lelland

Mrs Elizabeth M, 5
Lemoine
Avit, 2
Byron F, 1
Oscar, 2
Thomas L, 6
Leray
George E, 18
Leroy
Ernest, 72
Leveque
Mary J, 15
Lewis
Andrew J, 26
Charles, 60
Cordia I, 61
George C, 72
Leah, 21
Margaret B, 18
Mrs A, 72
Robert L, 73
William J, 71
Liles
Henry B, 58
John M, 58
Limbocker
Marcus N, 15
Lingard
Sam E, 9
Lisso
Roy M, 43
Livingston
Deborah, 35
Emanuel, 35
Lloyd
Rinda Ella, 53
Lockwood
Charles B, 63
Lofton
William M, 69
Long

Effie, 53
Myrtle K, 81
Lorrain
Louis, 15
Lovelace
Emma, 36
Miss Sallie, 35
Mrs Sallie E, 37
Loveland
Robert B, 55
Lovell
Lavenia Jane, 57
Lowdermilk
Lillard, 80
Lucas
John L, 79
Joseph P, 77
Luce
Jonathan N, 34
Luker
James, 50
Lutrell
William L, 55
Luttrick
Cornelius E, 31
W H, 31
Lyles
Cordelia, 47
Daniel P, 23
Hiram C, 10
William H, 46
Lyons
David A, 11
John L, 12
Machen
Henry E, 38, 80
Malachowsky
Joseph, 57
Mallett
Louis V, 49
Manning
Charles, 44

Manuel
 Raoul, 23
Marcotte
 Amelia, 1
 Ulysses J, 2
 Wilford B, 5
Mardis
 Alonzo F, 34
Marler
 James M, 54
Marner
 M M, 56
Marshall
 Bowman, 68
 Francis W, 44
 Mrs Emma V, 1
 Nellie A, 25
 William Branch, 1
Martin
 A L, 72
 Charles M C, 78
 Charles S, 65
 Oliver H, 36
 Oliver M, 39
 Seth, 65
Mason
 James M, 15
Massey
 William T, 55
Mathis
 J W, 75
 Thomas H, 80
Matthews
 J D, 24
 Ralph L, 38
Mayer
 Bernhardt, 46
 David, 48
 George L, 6
 Rosina W, 48
Mayes

Hugh V, 73
Mayo
 Elijah L, 64
 Elizabeth S, 64
 John R, 61
 Joseph O, 64
 Napoleon B, 64
Mazilly
 Louis E, 18
McCabe
 John H, 37
McCain
 Felix M, 74
McCalet
 William D, 63
McCarty
 Allen C, 76
 William H, 73
McClain
 Robert W, 64
McConathy
 Samuel, 27
McCraney
 John H, 55
McCullough
 James B, 66
 Samuel S, 68
McDonald
 William, 37
 William J, 59
McDougals
 Etta F, 41
McDowell
 Walter W, 80
McElveen
 Hattie M, 70
McFarlain
 Andew D, 14
 Andrew D, 14
McFatter
 Daniel W, 28
 Jesse L, 66

John E, 64
McGee
   William H, 65
McGraw
   Lydia R, 39
   William E, 39
McGuffie
   Robert F, 35
McKaskle
   Henry L, 73
   Jesse, 80
McKay
   Robert Lee, 33
McKennit
   Emma, 25
McKinney
   Miss Iva H, 44
McMahon
   James E, 16
McManus
   Hugh L, 67
McMillian
   George W, 80
McMillin
   Meda, 34
McNeal
   Cloyce M, 2
   John R, 2
   Zoe E, 2
McNichols
   Martha, 42
McQuatters
   Joseph J, 30
McVey
   Frank, 12
McWilliam
   John P, 25
Meadows
   Isaac S, 11
   John D, 74
   Mary M, 25
Mearns

William D, 15
Meek
   Jay W, 38
Meeker
   John L, 52
   Joseph H, 56
   Samuel F, 51
Melder
   Felix Van, 47
   Henry J, 53
   Henry L, 47
   Henry S, 49
Melder Jr
   John, 47
Melton
   Lamar L, 78
Melwick
   Ezekial P, 19
Mercer
   Jesse L, 52
Merchant
   J Webster, 53
Merrel
   Robert J, 55
Merrick
   William D, 7
Meyer
   Bernard D, 56
   William, 15
Michael
   Peter H, 81
Mickey
   Clarence C, 70
Midkiff
   Auda Flora, 60
   Florence C, 60
   Isaac W, 59
   Mary M, 59, 60
Miers
   Elias, 14, 22
Milbanks
   Joseph M, 52

Miles
- Charles J, 19
- Pleasant L, 33
- Whittle A, 28

Miller
- Cader C, 63
- Emily E, 53
- Harry H, 66
- John W, 43
- Levi A, 10
- Mrs Grover S, 18
- Peter K, 21
- Whitty S, 47
- William F, 34

Mills
- Frank M, 30
- William H, 38

Mills Jr
- William, 43

Millsaps
- Virgil L, 67

Mims
- Larkin M, 17

Mitcham
- Katie, 69
- Thomas F, 69

Mitchell
- J T, 38
- Thomas, 58
- William J, 11

Moffett
- William M, 73

Molloy
- Gilbert R, 21

Moncla
- Constant J, 8
- Ernest, 8
- Laura, 8
- Louis E, 8

Montgomery
- Charles J, 35

Earl H, 35
- Florence K, 34
- Joseph E, 34
- Stewart, 33

Moore
- Gertrude, 81
- John E, 21
- Martha A E, 17
- Patrick E, 13

Moreland
- Howard J, 34

Morgan
- Gordon, 7

Morgon
- Gordon, 7

Moritz
- Bernard, 37
- Leopold, 37

Morris
- Edward, 24
- Hadley R, 49
- Houston S, 76
- John H, 73
- Nathan D, 76
- William J, 49
- Willis M, 24

Morrison
- Edward I, 62
- Isaac A, 66
- Jesse L, 45, 59

Morrow
- Henry B, 70
- William E, 48

Morse
- John H, 45

Moseley
- Daisy, 34
- Daniel N, 24

Moss
- Lettie, 27
- Oliver R, 10

Perry
  Norman D, 17
  Norman J, 10
Peterson
  Bodine C, 55
  Rodin C, 55
Petty
  Don Green, 50
Phillips
  Charles J, 72
Philyan
  Maude, 28
Pickering
  Edward C, 64
Pickett
  Christianna L, 23
  Warren L, 23
Pierce
  Hazel V, 14
  Lula, 14
Piercy
  Morris G, 28
Pitre
  Willis A, 13
Pittmon
  Anette, 31
Pitts
  Auletus L, 17
Plauche
  Cyriaque B, 7
  Jean V, 7
Poe
  Benjamin E, 69
Ponder
  Henry O, 49
Poole
  Samuel C, 16
Post
  Herbert E, 25
Potts
  Rosebud, 28
Powell

Dewitt C, 12
Ezekial B, 75
Powers
  Angie F, 33
  Charles, 16
Powers Jr
  John T, 52
Pressburg
  Benjamin, 56
Price
  Frank G, 67
  George P, 41
  James B, 40
Pritchard
  John M, 35
Prothro
  H M, 74
Pruddhomme
  Virgie, 34
Puckett
  Joel D, 73
Pugh
  Tom, 72
Purifoy
  Charles E, 26
Purvis
  William T, 79
Rabalais
  Joseph H, 7
Rachall
  Rosa B, 46
Rand
  Edwin, 50
Randolph
  Benjamin H, 49
Randow
  Herman, 52
Ratcliff
  William G, 54
Raynolds
  David W, 9
Readheimer

114

Jessie Catherine, 66
Joseph G, 22
Martha, 22
Nettie H, 66
R W, 48
Willa H, 4
Whitehead
Julie, 35
Thomas P, 64
Wyatt M, 35
Whittington
Littleton P, 54
Whorton
William L, 78
Wiggington
James B, 34
Wilcocks
George, 16
Wilcox
Florence A, 44
Juliette, 16
Wiley
William, 53
Wilkinson
Jesse L, 76
Mrs Lee J, 73
Willar
James D, 11
William
Stephen D, 45
Williams
Benjamin F, 70
Edward L, 28
Henry A, 10
J R, 56
James L, 13
Jane R, 72
Joseph W, 45
Mrs Mary M, 45
Nathaniel S, 60
R E, 9

Rebecca, 46
Samuel S, 70
Thomas J, 63
William D, 60
Williamson
Mrs Eliza A, 20
Willis
Jessie B, 61
Wilson
G V, 46
Gordon V, 51
John B, 75
John M, 38
Wimberly
Cole H, 28
Mims W, 69
Windham
August P, 16
Harvey B, 67
Winegeart
William, 57
Winfree
A G, 61
Isaac O, 61
Winfrey
Jacob, 65
Wing
Giles M, 24
Wingate
Laban, 11
Thomas C, 58
Thomas E, 13
Wise
Noah, 50
Witherwax
Dock, 26
Wohl
Louis, 35
Wood
Alice H, 47
Mitchell M, 21

www.ingramcontent.com/pod-product-compliance
Lightning Source LLC
Chambersburg PA
CBHW070253290326
41930CB00041B/2502